GO FISHING FOR

BASS

GO FISHING FOR

BASS

GRAEME PULLEN

The Oxford Illustrated Press

© 1990, Graeme Pullen

ISBN 0 946609 90 X

Published by:
The Oxford Illustrated Press Limited, Haynes Publishing Group,
Sparkford, Nr Yeovil, Somerset BA22 7JJ, England.

Haynes Publications Inc, 861 Lawrence Drive, Newbury Park,
California 91320, USA.

Printed in England by:
J. H. Haynes & Co Limited, Sparkford, Nr Yeovil, Somerset.

British Library Cataloguing in Publication Data:
Pullen, Graeme
    Go Fishing for bass.
    1. Great Britain. Fish: Bass. Angling – Manuals
    I. Title
    ISBN 0-946609-90-X

Library of Congress Catalog Card Number:
    89-80717

All photos from the author's files, 'Fishpix'.

Contents

Acknowledgements

Mr Norman Dunlop, Central Fisheries Board, Eire.

Dedication

To those who first wrote about the beauty
of the Irish bass strands.

Introduction

There is a fish swimming in European waters that has all the lines and markings of a fine sporting fish. Its mouth, predatorial and expansive; its eye, unforgettable and haunting. Its tail fin powerful yet quick in the pursuit of prey and its solid silver flank of scales shining like burnished armour ready for battle. The bass probably has more of a cult following among sea anglers than any other species. Unfortunately it is sought after not just by fishermen with rods but by commercial fishermen with nets and trawls. At the time of writing, the flesh of the bass is being sold for the staggering sum of £7.25 per pound in Harrod's, London—more expensive than salmon. Such a high market value means that very few commercial fishermen ever return a bass to the sea and in such a money-conscious world it is not hard to see why.

Even rod and line anglers sometimes sell their catch to defray travelling and other expenses, putting additional pressure on a species that lives in localised areas and has a very slow growth rate. Assisted by high-tech, marine-electronic fish finding gear, commercial fishermen are able to wipe out entire stocks of bass in one fell swoop—the true rod and line sportsman barely scratching the surface of these clearly defined fish stocks. High financial incentive casts common sense to the wind. The opinion seems to be, catch them now while you can—if you don't, somebody else will.

The heart of bass fishing as a sport must surely rest with the shore fisherman. It is unlikely a man armed with a 12 ft beach rod is going to deplete bass stocks, especially if he is conservation minded and returns them to the sea. Keep one for eating if you must but safeguard your threatened sport by putting bass back if they are small to medium in size.

Despite the merits of bass fishing, the fighting quality of the fish is largely overrated. On light tackle it certainly gives a good account of itself, with a head-shaking movement that jars right down to the reel fitting. On heavy boat gear, however, you can haul bass out on pirks and feathers, but it would hardly be deemed 'sport'.

There are various methods to fish bass from both boat and shore, but the optimum must surely be to fish a creaming Irish surf beach, or strand, where the tables of water foam three layers out and you can see green water as the sunlight dances on a curling wave. To get a

7

good surf up you need some wind and many anglers do not like being uncomfortable, but if you want the best of the shore bass, you will have to put up with wind! The culmination of fishing for this species is the sight of that glaring eye and erect dorsal fin bristling with spines as you drag it unceremoniously through the last few feet of water. It is everything a fish should be. Its feeding habits can be finicky or downright bold as it almost pulls the rod from your fingers. The take may come immediately the bait or lure hits the water, or it may come after hours spent watching a motionless rod top. Often with bass fishing it does not come at all. They can be secretive as they nose between rock gullies filled by a quietly flooding tide, or they can churn the surface amid a screaming flock of terns as they feed on small fish.

Anglers have caught bass since time began and it would be easy to say that they will always be there. Unfortunately, however, I feel we are already on an irreversible downwards slide. Aside from commercial over exploitation, I think there may be a problem with fry survival due to the continuing use of the sea as a bottomless pit for pollutants and effluents. (Already we have seen the massive mortality rate amongst seals in the North Sea, possibly brought about by heavy metal pollutants and PCB, a product reported as early as 1977 by scientists on the East Coast of America. First we have the commercial overkill of mature fish, which leaves less adult bass to replenish their kind and then, if they *do* have a successful spawning, pollution takes its toll and prevents many of their fry reaching maturity. A catch-22 situation due entirely to man's intervention.

The bass is a proud warrior that deserves a fighting chance of survival. In this book, I only intend to give you a few tips learnt from personal experience on how to catch them. I cannot give you exact locations for fear of them being exploited commercially. All I suggest you do is try bass fishing for yourself. They are superb fish and may be one of the first to suffer near extinction from our coastline. Try fishing for them as soon as you can and should you be fortunate enough to enjoy a good day, keep one, keep two, but please, don't keep them all.

Introduction

Profile of a bass. A large eye and a cavernous mouth are the signs of a true ocean predator. They can be fickle creatures and a careful note of their haunts and habits is the best way of ensuring that they find their way to the end of your line.

Bass Research

In its heyday, the south-west coast of Ireland probably boasted the finest surf fishing for bass in Europe. The early 1960s brought top-class fishing but also an influx of tourist anglers keen to catch bass in majestic surroundings. This west corner of Ireland is probably still one of the least polluted areas in the North Atlantic. However, angling successes bring commercial pressure, and the bass stocks started to decline. The Inland Fisheries Trust, now the Central Fisheries Board, set about researching the demise of the bass which in turn had an adverse effect on the tourist trade. My thanks go to Norman Dunlop of the Central Fisheries Board for allowing me to use some information from their paper, *Some Observations on the Life History of the Bass* by P. Fitzmaurice.

The bass is a southern European/North African species, and Ireland is near the northern limit of its range. Indeed, the geographical range in Ireland shows clearly that the species is more abundant in the southern part of the country. As a general rule they are more prolific below a line drawn approximately from Galway to Wexford. Their frequent occurrence in these areas appears to be temperature related, the sea temperature on the southern coast of Ireland being on average 2 °C warmer than the sea temperatures on the northern coasts. In spring, summer and autumn the bass are found in estuaries and creeks, in the bays into which rivers flow and on sandy beaches, especially in the vicinity of river mouths, streams and headlands. They can run into very shallow water. Only recently on a trip to Co. Kerry, I came across a small river running onto a strand with only a few feet of water at high water springs. When a good surf was up those bass were right in the channel of the stream, in water that was scarcely three feet deep. Although the standard lugworms presented on the bottom were refused, we had crashing runs from bass on sandeels. I assume they were attracted to the vicinity of the stream mouth by the freshwater—they have a fairly high tolerance of brackish and freshwater. I even remember bass being caught on the Royalty fishery of the Hampshire Avon River at Christchurch which was certainly the home of freshwater species. The huge River Shannon in Ireland is tidal to just above Limerick, some 45 miles from the open sea, and bass have been reported as far up the river as the entry point of the River Fergus, some 30 miles from the open sea. Other areas have also seen the bass range regularly as far upriver as 10 miles or more. It is thought that the presence of food, in terms of crabs and shrimps, dictates this distance.

With prices currently retailing at up to £7.25 per pound, the bass is an expensive fish and this box is worth a good deal. Small wonder that few fish are returned—increasing the pressure on this slow growing species.

Go Fishing for Bass

The main worry with regard to the overfishing of the Irish stocks in the 1960s was the slow replacement time. Bass are very slow growing and have a clearly defined size range which covers the largest and smallest mature fish. In Irish waters, male bass attain sexual maturity within 4 to 7 years, and females within 5 to 8 years. The females also outnumber the male stocks in the ratio of about 2 to 1. As for spawning seasons, the examination of gonads in large bass indicate that spawning time occurs mainly in the months of May and June. Active, mature males have been found as early as February on the Kerry coast, and as late as June in other areas. Again, I feel that sea water temperatures must play a fairly crucial part in the spawning requirements of this species. A bass caught at Stradbally strand on the Dingle peninsula of Co. Kerry was found to have nearly 410,000 eggs, but of course only a tiny fraction of those can survive the natural predation system of inland coastal waters. The species have been spawned artificially in aquariums in both Naples and Plymouth, so possibly there may be a case in the future for this species being reared like trout, restocking with wild fish. The main drawback to a venture such as this is the slow growth rate in comparison to feed and management stock costs.

As part of the Irish programme researching the decline of their bass fishery, tow-netting for eggs was undertaken. It was thought that mature stocks would be concentrated in an area of high egg distribution but the technique had only limited success. In order to get some idea of the effect of the tidal current on the drift of eggs, a few surface drift bottles were released in 1970 in Blasket Sound and at the Splaugh rock, where eggs had in fact been obtained. Two out of the 7 bottles released in Blasket Sound were found and reported. Both were picked up within a few miles of each other at Ballyheigh, Co. Kerry, in the angle formed by Kerry Head and Banna Strand. They had drifted about 35 miles over a period of 5 and 6 days respectively. Banna Strand is an area of surf beach that I have always felt was a good food holding area, with possibilities of big bass, and the path of these drift bottles appears to confirm my thinking. The bottles released at the Splaugh rock towards the south-east of Ireland yielded no useful results, except to prove that the sea currents pushed them as far as Anglesey and the Menai Strait. A subsequent release of drift bottles at Tuskar Rock confirmed this movement, and indicates that perhaps the North Atlantic drift current actually parts somewhere like Cork to push up North and Westwards with its warm water, leaving cooler water to run up East and North of the coast of Ireland.

The Central Fisheries Board in Ireland is responsible for much of the information provided about the bass species. This fish has been tagged ready for return to the sea—the Floy tag is in position just behind the dorsal fin.

In Ireland, very young bass enter the nursery areas of low to middle reaches of estuaries and tidal creeks of a fairly high salinity. They seldom occur in any large numbers on the open surf beaches, presumably because of the easier availability of food in quieter waters. Both scales and the operculars (gill bone covers), can be used to determine the age of the bass. As an indication of their slow growth rate, the largest bass whose scales were examined was a female weighing 17 lb 1^{1}/4 oz, landed at Whiting Bay, Co.

Go Fishing for Bass

Waterford. It was 21 years old which, for a fish of any species, is a long time to elude the many nets of advanced commercial fishermen. Other bass have had their age determined accurately: up to 16 years in Clifden, Co. Galway, and 14 years in Youghal, Co. Cork. The males, as a rule do not grow as fast as the females, and tend not to live as long. It was also discovered that, from a total of 176 large bass recorded, 133 had been caught in the south-west region on baits, and only 85 in the south-eastern region on lures. This may have been due to the south-west corner of the country being warmer and having a longer tourist season.

While the scale readings did not afford any definite sign of regional differences in the growth of Irish bass, there were certainly

This is one of the biggest bass ever caught from the shore. Ken Flack's massive 17 lb 2¹/2 oz bass came from a mark near his home in Bridgwater, Somerset. Few anglers ever see this size of fish and to catch one from the shore is quite exceptional. Photograph courtesy of Ken Flack.

14

indications that bass grow faster in some years than in others. This is known as year classing, when spawning may also be particularly successful, yielding a high survival rate, and thus leaving a higher percentage of bass to reach bigger weights. Way back in 1959 it was noticed that the year class was larger than average even at the end of the first season.

Bass other than specimens have been recorded into two groups. Bass caught during the years 1947-63 made all or most of their growth during the 40s and 50s, while the 1959 year class made up nearly half the stocks of adult bass present on the Irish coast in 1967 and 1968. The 1947-63 bass stocks made better growth than the 1959 class, mainly due to the lower than average sea temperatures in the early 1960s. I remember well a couple of the big freeze-ups we had in this period, which must have severely damaged not only growth rates of bass stocks existing at the time but any spawning that managed to take place. As sea temperature obviously plays such a crucial part in spawning and growth rates, I believe there may well be a case for blaming the mid-1960s decline of the bass not entirely on commercial over-exploitation but also on poor spawning years. By the mid-1960s, when sea temperatures had stabilised, the spawning maintained a higher success level and we should be getting some good fish from the post-1960 years' classes, and indeed there have been some good fish recorded around the British Isles. The growing popularity of fishing, modern tackle and refined techniques may mean larger bass will be caught but a good spawning year will undoubtedly mean that more fish are available.

The pattern of growth rate implies that bass situated in waters in the northern extremes of their range, such as the coast around Northern Ireland, have a longer life span but suffer much slower growth rates, while those in warmer waters like the Atlantic coast of Morocco grow very fast but live for shorter periods. This has been confirmed by routine sampling and analysis of bass in the northern waters, with fish up to 19 years old, and bass in French waters even reaching 30 years of age. A 20 lb bass in French waters may be 20 to 25 years old, similar to Irish and English statistics. The oldest fish examined at the southern geographical range was 87 cm in length yet was aged at only 13 years.

Go Fishing for Bass

It is often thought that all bass are shoal fish. Where baitfish predominate, such as the whitebait shoals around the Splaugh rock, then the bass will pursue them right up to the surface—ideal for the angler using artificial lures. In other coastal regions there may be an abundance of sandeels, a major source of food for bass, and again bass will congregate to cash in on this food source. Where food is not concentrated, bass will resort to eating almost anything and will come extremely close to rocky shores in their foraging for food. A list of the stomach contents found in a typical bass included: sea trout, sandeels, herring fry, flounders, brill, blenny, butterfish, stickleback, sea scorpion, shore crabs, edible crabs, prawns, shrimps, lugworms, ragworms, bivalves, and sea anemones. Few could be regarded as angler's baits. Bass spawning in the spring produce only lean fish but summer and autumn feeding will see these fish put on fat, pushing them into prime condition by early October. Females tend to be heavier than males for their length.

Bass are localised species but they do have some seasonal migrations. They appear to leave the estuaries and river mouths in late October or early November, when the sea temperatures start to fall from 13 to 14 °C to 8 to 10 °C. Few bass are then taken from the shore until the following spring. However, in areas like Dingle Bay where the sea temperatures stay warmer the bass can be caught as early as February. In the 1988 season, the skipper of the *Skua*, George Burgum, wrote to me advising that anglers were catching numbers of bass from the back of Inch Strand in February, although of course the 1988 winter was one of the mildest recorded. Bass have been caught during periods of fine weather on hand lines in Youghal Bay, and Salmon netsmen take the occasional bass in Youghal Bay in February and March. While this would indicate that the species does not move far from the shore, they obviously do go somewhere in the colder months, possibly to deep water. A tagged bass was taken in a trawl 3 miles east of the Saltee Islands in about 20 fathoms of water. The massive reduction in the number of anglers fishing for bass in winter as compared to the summer and autumn months must also result in less fish being caught.

Tagging has revealed a little more about bass movements. From 1967-78 inclusive, 1053 adult and 28 juvenile bass were tagged on the

16

Bass Research

You can't always guarantee you'll catch bass even when you do everything right. This angler looks happy with a brace of surf-caught flounders that fell to a two-hook lug-baited rig intended for bass.

Irish coast. All the fish were caught on rod and line, mostly by Inland Fisheries Trust staff, and the remainder by some 20 anglers co-operating with the tagging programme. The original tag in use was made from laminated colourless cellulose acetate containing a message on one side and a number on the other. By using a hypodermic needle they were attached to the fish with 20-lb test-braided Terylene fishing line. During 1978, Floy tags were used on an experimental basis and it appears that these gave much better returns. Tags which had been on bass for up to 12 months were reported to be still firmly attached. Bass recaptured during the same year were, in general, taken within 10 miles of where they were marked. One bass however, tagged in Ballyteigue Bay, travelled 80 miles to Garrettstown Strand, Co. Cork, in just 82 days. Two bass marked in the spring on Kerry beaches travelled 42 miles to the Shannon Estuary in 14 days, and 26 miles to the Cashen Estuary in

14 days. Two bass marked in Dungarvan in late September were recaptured in the Waterford Estuary, 39 miles away, one after 6 days, the other after 35 days. Perhaps this is a sign that the species is moving down from its northern limit on the west coast and working its way around the south end of the country as the sea temperature starts to drop. Seven bass were recaptured in the location of the original tagging and the longest period a fish had been at liberty was 386 days. This fish was tagged on the Wexford coast and recaptured the following year in the same place.

Tagging research confirms, therefore, that although the bass may sweep in and out of estuaries and travel surf beaches with each passing tide, it still remains relatively localised. Most of the tagged fish were recaptured within 18 miles of where they were released, a clear indication of the best area for commercial fishermen to concentrate their efforts.

I have already said that the bass is extremely susceptible to over fishing and the following report provides additional proof: out of 6 recaptures from 84 fish marked at Blackhall Strand, Co. Wexford, 5 were subsequently recaptured on the very same strand and by the same angler. Couple this with the fact that bass need an extensive nursery area in unpolluted brackish or estuarine waters and it is easy to see how threatened they are as a species. Their tendency to roam into freshwater streams and rivers that enter the sea brings them into contact with any farm pollution that may run down from the river. This pollution of nursery areas and the detrimental effect these polluted waters have on bass has been borne out by scientists in the United States reporting on the demise of their own striped bass.

Striped Bass

The striped bass is a North American species very similar to our European bass but it grows to the tremendous size of 100 lb. The prolific research undertaken in the United States provides us with much of the latest information with which to draw conclusions about our own bass and I therefore think it is worth closing this chapter with a section on the habits and conditions of the striped bass.

The females may live to 40 years of age, the slower growing males having a shorter life span. Having fished for 'stripers' on both the Outer Banks of North Carolina and the freshwater lakes of Utah, I can vouch that they are just as streamlined and exciting as our own species.

If you think European bass fishermen are dedicated enthusiasts, you might want to hear about the striped bass fisherman who has to be a real fanatic. He is a man who spends hours slipping and sliding down mud creeks in pursuit of an elusive grey shape in the water; or hangs around jetties and piers staring into the depths. He spends so much time fishing the beaches he eventually exhausts himself, grabs a few hours sleep, then hits the beaches again. His mode of transport is a fully-customised 4-wheel drive vehicle, which enables him to scour every sandbank, wave and depression along the miles of sandy beach.

The striped bass has a unique following among American shore fishermen. It is a species rated by the International Game Fishing Association (IGFA) as a gamefish. As long ago as 1643 the bass was written about as a fighting fish that was also fine to eat. During the 1870s a number of famous striped bass fishing clubs were formed. Among these were such colourful names as the Cuttyhunk Club, the Squibnocket, Pasque Island, West Island and Cohasset Narrows. One strange factor common to many clubs was that they often kept a large roost of pigeons. These were used for communication with the mainland, in order to tell members carrying on their business that the stripers were 'in', and ready to bite. Most of the famous striped bass fishing clubs disintegrated when the species unaccountably almost disappeared at the beginning of this century. Then, just as quickly as they vanished, they hit the Atlantic east coast in 1936, creating a major revival of the species. A similar strange incident had occurred in 1879. A number of striped bass, mostly small fish, were seine netted in the Navesink River in New Jersey, then transported across the continent to San Francisco bay. Only 435 fish survived the trip but 20 years later the commercial catch of stripers alone reached 1,234,000 lb!

Considering the limited equipment used way back then, it was a most amazing haul and indicates just how well a striped bass can

adapt to a change in environment. To illustrate this further there is the case of the non-migratory stripers that remained in the drainage area of Santee-Cooper in South Carolina. They have always lived there, but after the construction of two giant dams they were unable to reach saltwater. Now they are landlocked and even breed very successfully. This was noted by many freshwater fishermen, who realised the striped bass could be one of the biggest species to be caught on lures and baits. Stripers were introduced to many of the large inland water reservoirs in America, and so too were the food fish to sustain them.

Stripers have a prodigious appetite, and if they are going to flourish they need a good supply of live food. To stop them eating everything else in the reservoirs, biologists first introduced thousands of threadfin shad into the water systems. When these had bred and become established, the stripers were introduced and grew with such a fantastic rate that people began talking about the possibilities of a freshwater striped bass breaking the existing world record, which was held in saltwater. The world record is over 70 lb, and already the freshwater stripers have been logged to 50 lb. It seems only a matter of time before a new record is reported. The recurring problem, however, is that they can actually eat themselves out of existence. If there is a shortfall in the shad population it affects the stripers immediately.

I have been to 'striper' country several times, both to the coast of North Carolina where beach buggies line the surf of the outer banks, and to the huge bodies of inland water like Lake Powell. When I fished there in 1987, fishermen were noting that the stripers in the 3–10 lb range were looking lean and hungry. They were eating their way through the shad population, even on a reservoir which is 189 miles long! I still managed to catch them, although their usual haunts seemed empty of fish and we had to search around. Striped bass are a superb species in both fresh and saltwater and while I should like to

Left: The striped bass could well be a species to boost our own flagging European bass stocks. This striper weighed 54 lb 8 oz and was taken on 20-lb line by Herman King. The world record all-tackle striped bass was in fact taken from the shore and weighed a staggering 78 lb 8 oz. The lucky angler won the largest amount of money ever paid for a single fish when he heard about a competition being sponsored by Abu-Garcia that was offering a quarter of a million dollars for an all-tackle record striper. Photograph courtesy of IGFA.

see them stocked over here, the chances are unlikely although I feel sure they would flourish and help to replace the dwindling stocks of European bass we have left today. There would probably be an outcry that they would take the food of other species but they are arguably a more worthwhile species to have in the water. No doubt they would become commercially viable and I suppose we all know what the commercial fishermen would do if they got their gill nets around striped bass. The species would be fished virtually to extinction, like our own bass have been.

Should any stocking of small stripers be undertaken, I would like to see it happen in Irish waters. Here the commercial pressure is somewhat less and the environment would be well suited to them. Rocky headlands, huge estuaries, rivers and wide open surf beaches in which they could breed and hunt. I have no idea whether they could inter-breed with our own European bass, but it may well be possible as they have a hybrid, though sterile, cross in the States between the striper and the white bass.

As a final indication of the potential available with this species, one of the largest ever netted was a massive 125-lb striper in the mouth of the Chowan River. If of course you get the chance to travel to the Outer Banks of North Carolina I should advise you that the really big stripers are few in number. Pollution in one of their major spawning areas, Chesapeake Bay, has been blamed for the dwindling stocks, but even so you will find the American surf fisherman very hospitable and keen to give you information and tips on areas to fish, the baits to use and the most suitable rigs. The nearest I can suggest is Oregon Inlet, Nag's Head or Hatteras Point. Professional guides are available for hire, complete with a 4-wheel drive and tackle with a live-bait well on the front fender. I have fished with Joe Malat, a friendly guide and excellent at finding his clients a good place to try. One thing he cannot do however, is put the fish on the hook for you and neither, despite the tips in this book, can I!

The need for well-researched information on dwindling bass stocks in this country has never been more urgent. Only armed with facts and figures can bass fishermen successfully lobby the government and put pressure on them to pass tougher laws to conserve this superb species for future generations.

Baits

Whatever the species of fish, I am continually asked the same question: 'What do you really consider to be the very best bait Graeme?' As far as shore fishing for bass is concerned, I can only put forward opinions that are not only my own but also those of other bass enthusiasts.

Crabs

The crab at first sight is a pretty unsophisticated creature. Yet the humble crab, when properly fished, is easily the most successful bass bait, certainly for fish in excess of 3 lb in weight. For the small school bass of 1-2 lb, worms or lures can be more productive, depending on the feeding situation at the time. A fallacy held by a great many shore anglers is that it is only the peeler crab, with its soft, outer shell, that bass eat. Not at all. Bass eat green hardback shore crabs just as quickly as they scoop up anything else. Remember that during the stage of 'peeling' the crab realises its vulnerability to predation, and spends most of that period hiding beneath rocks and weed. I hardly think the bass goes round turning over boulders just to get at the soft crab; it's the anglers that are responsible, in their quest to get this bait.

The crab most likely to be of interest to the bass angler is the common green shore crab. This grows to approximately four inches across its shell, has a dark green back, and is distinguished from the

Go Fishing for Bass

Peeler crabs are usually found below the high water mark, beneath rocks and boulders. Here Essex angler Mick Redding, who has landed bass to over 11 lb, searches the rocks for soft peeler crabs.

edible crab by its green colour. The edible crab will have a pink to light rusty brown hue to its shell and grows substantially larger, up to eight inches or more across its shell. Another species undoubtedly eaten by the bass is the hermit crab, again a good source of bait for shore anglers. You can get these from trawlers' nets as a by-product catch, or even from lobster potters. Other species include the fiddler or velvet swimming crab, the masked crab, the furrowed crab, the pea crab and the immature spider crabs. Of all these, the pea crab is the one most likely to be taken on a regular basis by a shore feeding bass. They are really too small to be considered as a potential bait by serious shore fishermen, but I have heard of them being floatfished on light tackle around piers and from jetties for school bass. Start by collecting the green shore crab in its peeling stage. This requires a thorough search of any rocky shoreline, but I should point out that judging a good crabbing ground does demand some experience. You rarely get good crabs from the slate-bed type of rock, or where geologically the solid rock continues right down into the sea. Sometimes there will be an area of thick kelp over the hard rock, and there will be crabs in this but it is rare to find them in the peeling stage in this area.

What you need is an area that offers lots of broken rocks, boulders, slabs and large stones—anything with a lip or edge that the crab can get underneath. There is no easy way of sorting out this ground. You simply have to get in there and go over each rock systematically. What you are looking for is the soft green crab, so just pick them up, check with a squeeze to see if the shell is soft, and drop them back if it's hard. Another way to tell if the crab is about to peel if you are unsure how soft it is, is to twist off a segment of leg. If it comes away leaving the meat beneath, then the crab should be kept as it will be in the process of peeling. If the leg breaks off, the meat is still attached to the shell, and it's just a common green shore crab. Any limb broken off will soon grow back. I don't suggest you do this with every single crab you find, just the odd one that you think might be a peeler.

My own theory regarding the tremendous success rate of the peeler crab relates to the fact that when the crab is in the process of shedding its shell to replace it with another new one, body juices are released into the surrounding area. Indeed a third way to test a crab to see if it's a peeler, is to look for soapy bubbles coming out from around the side and underneath the shell when you squeeze it. The crab blows itself up with seawater to throw the old shell off and grow the new one, which means the body juices must be diluted into the surrounding water. Small wonder that all manner of species are intent on locating the source of the scent!

Many good areas for shore bassing are devoid of rocks and it would therefore seem likely the bass just feed on worm baits. This is no doubt the case, especially on wide mudflats, but crabs will still move in and out with the tides. They presumably go through the act of peeling in the shelter of the deeper water beyond the low tide mark, but still provide a source of food at high water. With no rocks or boulders to hide under, the peeler crabs need to be provided with a sanctuary. Two items are popular with anglers, especially in the north-east of England, where peeler collecting has become something of a fine art. Old tyres stacked flat provide an excellent refuge for crabs to hide in. Also lengths of old plastic drainpipe laid out allow crabs in and are easy to empty. However as both tyres and plastic drainpipes are not biodegradable, I don't suggest you throw them all over the place. Professional crab collectors often keep an area to themselves, or they may move all the crabs traps with each tide. Don't make the mistake of going round trying to steal the peelers from somebody else's traps. Professional crab collectors are already wise to that and place razor blades and broken glass inside their traps to minimise pilfering.

I have heard of peeler crabs being kept in a temperature controlled aquarium and while it is no problem to keep hardbacks in tanks, the peelers are in a more fragile state. As soon as a peeler dies it must be removed otherwise it infects the whole of the tank's occupants and ultimately kills them. In general, it is best to keep the crabs alive in a bucket of wet seaweed in a cool place. One thing that does come in handy is a silver bait pouch as used by pike fishermen for keeping their baits frozen. This is a small sachet that you can drop several crabs into, certainly enough for a day's bassing, allowing the baits to stay cool. Yet another, and larger accessory is the ASW Coolfishbag marketed in England. In the smaller size, this high quality product

Baits

Probably the best bait for the shore bass enthusiast—a peeler crab expertly held on a hook with black elasticated thread and the hook-point exposed. Make sure that the hook is always exposed otherwise it will sink into the bait on striking rather than into the bass's jaw.

can be used to keep all your baits cool, and it comes complete with a removable inner lining and ample carrying straps. The idea is to put some freezer blocks into the lining, place your baits in a tupperware or bait box inside, and zip the top shut. It keeps peelers frozen if dead, or chilled if live, and of course you should always be using the freshest possible bait.

Two things that do not work well together are peeler crabs and long-distance casting. As previously mentioned, a crab in its peeling state will be very soft. It's not possible just to thread it up a hookshank and let it fly with a powerful cast. If it doesn't fall off on the beach it explodes like a firework about 50 ft up! At night you may not see this happen and could be fishing a cast out with no bait at all on the hook. What you need is a special crab hook and some

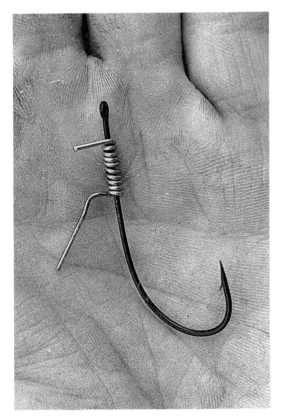

A customised crab hook as used by the author and other bass anglers. Wind the paperclip wire around the shank of the hook as illustrated and then impale the crab on the longer, sloping spike and hold in position with elasticated thread. The thread is tied off on the smaller, vertical 'pin' which means it can be tied less tightly ensuring that the important crab juices are not squeezed out. This also prevents the hook-point being masked by the crab's body when you strike.

elasticated thread to whip it on with. Despite my sending a converted hook design made by anglers to a manufacturer in the hope that they may mass produce it, they have yet to come up with a shop bought model. There are versions about called crab hooks but basically they are just wider in the gape to accommodate the crab's body. They don't have any retaining spine on which to slot the crab. Almost any hook can be made into a customised crab hook by simply winding some paper clip wire around the shank. This is best done at home on those windy, wet evenings when you can't get out. You can see from the photograph what it looks like. Basically you have an angled piece of wire onto which you push the crab's body. This acts as a main support. You should also have a small vertical piece of wire which you can wind the elasticated thread onto. This thread need not be knotted but will bind down tight enough for casting and then snap off. When a crab is used in this way it can either be lobbed out 200 ft or used with a bait-retaining clip and blasted out well over 300 ft and still remain intact. A fiddly job but one well worth doing when fishing peeler crabs.

Sandeels

While the peeler crab must be the undisputed favourite bait of the shore angler, the sandeel must be the best bet for those wishing to fish from a boat. Having said that, this little sliver of silver can be devastating from the shore as well. The reason for not classing it first for shore baits is that the peeler has the ability to catch bass in dirty water, such as the Bristol Channel and Thames Estuary, whereas the sandeel definitely works best in cleaner waters such as surf beaches. As described previously, the peeler obviously exudes a lot of body juices when it expands to push off its shell. The sandeel must give off some sort of scent trail but being prolific only in the cleanest of waters, and having an incredible turn of speed, I feel they are primarily visual baits for the bass. You can ledger them on the bottom if fishing from a beach, or floatfish them live off headlands and rocks. If you can keep them alive then do so—your chances of a take then increase dramatically.

Go Fishing for Bass

Prime bait for inshore bass fishing. A live sandeel should be lightly hooked in the belly with the trace running through the membrane of its lower jaw. Hooked like this, sandeels stay alive for a considerable period of time.

Let's deal with the live sandeel first. There are two ways to get hold of them: you can either dig or rake them yourself from the beach, or buy them live from a professional sandeel netter. Certainly for the amount it should cost you to buy them, a few pounds, I would buy them live whenever possible. The professional netter will keep them alive in a wooden penner or courge. This is simply a triangular box, made of wood so that it floats, with small holes drilled in it to ensure a flow of fresh seawater. Provided these holes do not clog up with seaweed the eels will stay alive for days. If you are using them immediately, or transferring them to a boat with its own live well, you can transport them in a bucket of wet seaweed. On no account use freshwater, which will kill them off. There are plenty of places around Cornwall and Devon that will provide you with live sandeels but if you travel further afield you may have to get your own. This entails raking or digging them from the beach, and I assure you it's no easy task! This will be the method used most by beach anglers to obtain their eels and I should point out that the times for getting them are strictly limited. The only places you find them are in areas of small shingle, washed clean by the tide, and at the low water line.

Digging for live sandeels is hard work—note the number of anglers watching this poor chap!

The very best time for digging eels is at low water springs, when the tide goes out to its farthest, but also comes in at its quickest. This doesn't leave much time so if you do decide to dig them, you need an abundance of enthusiasm coupled with lightning reflexes. Turn the shingle over, one spit deep, almost as fast as you can, watching like a hawk for any sandeels that are thrown up. At first they are surprised at the disturbance but it only takes them about a second to realise what is going on and they immediately zip back into the shingle. Once below the surface they can wriggle down faster than you can dig, so save your effort for new ground rather than dig feverishly after a lost cause. I pounce on mine as soon as I see them, trying not to grab the sandeel but to grab a handful of grit around the outside of the eel which prevents it slipping away. They are like quicksilver but catch them fresh like this and you have one of the best baits for bassing. Should you be close to a river or estuary, then look for these finely washed gravel sand or stone beds at the very lowest water mark. Take care not to get cut off—seek local advice first if the tide has a high rise and fall area. Presumably this finely washed gravel has plenty of oxygen flowing through it from the seawater, for I have never yet dug sandeels from sand frequented by the lug and ragworm. This fine gravel is another reason why they vanish as soon as you dig them.

If you intend using them dead, then simply throw them in a bucket or container, but make sure it has steep sides, or better still a lid, so they can't wriggle away. Nothing is worse than seeing 2 or 3 sandeels flip out of the container after you have moved half a ton of gravel to get them. Should you intend keeping them alive you will need a good-sized bait bucket which should be filled almost to the top with fresh seawater, not freshwater. If you have a lid of some sort so much the better. A shop-bought aerator pump like the Shakespeare model, powered by a couple of batteries, provides enough oxygen to keep them alive all day if the bait is to be used on the same session. Any sandeels damaged by 'forking' should be kept separate, and perhaps frozen down for later use. If you want to keep them for several days, and this is always a hazardous affair as they suffer a high mortality rate, then put them in a saltwater aquarium. Some anglers also have an attachment in their car enabling them to keep their pump running from a socket placed into the cigarette lighter until they reach their venue. Then they use the portable battery model.

A final word on digging or raking sandeels: start digging as soon as the water has left the gravel beds, following it down as you dig and keeping as close to the low water mark as possible. Low water spring tides are the best so you will need to work hard in a short period of time. If the area is washed by strong currents it may have formed ridges or humps. You should find most of the sandeels on the seaward side of the humps, so concentrate your efforts on that area first. Don't go crazy—take a rest now and then, as you need half your strength for grabbing the little blighters before they wriggle back.

Profile of a bass. A carefully placed artificial will take bass successfully.

Above left: Peeler crabs, ready to use and one of the greatest all-round bass baits. Tied with elasticated cotton, they can be clipped down with a bait clip and cast without them breaking up.

Above right: Using either peeler crabs or lugworm, you can land both bass and flounder on the same cast—two species that run open surf beaches together.

Left: Lugworm, a very popular surf bait for bass.

On his first bass fishing trip to Ireland with the author, Adrian Hutchins soon found that bass were attracted to his lugworm bait. There is still good fishing to be had in Ireland.

This lean shore bass of over 8 lb fell to a whole king ragworm fished from the low water mark at Hinckley Point power station. The Bristol channel yields some of the biggest shore bass in the British Isles.

A superb bass with its proud captor taken off St Catherine's Deeps by the Isle of Wight.

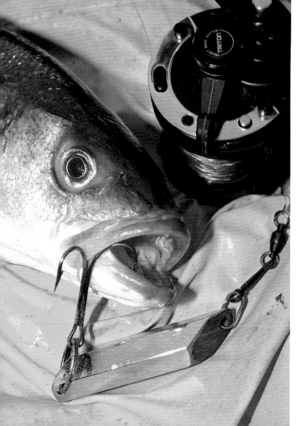

Above left: Lesser sandeels can either be netted, raked or dug. They are prime bass baits, particularly for the fisherman working in clear water conditions from a boat or from the shore.

Above right: Large ragworm are highly effective in specific areas, notably along the south coast of England and in the Bristol Channel. They seldom work well in regions where lugworm are prolific.

Left: The mini-pirk comes into its own in late spring when bass are concentrating on hunting out whitebait shoals.

The author unhooks a fine bass taken on lugworm fished in the fourth table of surf from Inch Strand in County Kerry. Don't cast out too far as bass often work in only eighteen inches of water.

A brace of bass landed by the author using mini pirks from the boat *4 Pints*.

Baits

If you are using the eels in a boat, the best method is to rig them on a long flowing trace, using a running ledger and just enough lead to hold bottom. If you fish them live, just take the hook in through the mouth, out through the lower jaw membrane and nick the hook point in through the skin of the stomach. This way they stay alive longest. While commercial netting primarily brings in sandeels, you may have acquired some really big sandeel while out feathering for mackerel. These are the greater sandeels, or launce as they are known. They rarely come in to the shallow waters of a surf beach, and are more likely to be found around rocky headlands. For the average sized bass of 3–4 lb, they are going to be too big, but if you have some anyway, why not try cutting them in half and using either a tail or head section? The tail section seems slightly more successful and I wonder if that's because the last thing a chasing bass sees when it hunts sandeels is the tail? In contrast, should you wish to cast from the shore, the eels can be frozen down in sections and taken to the beach in either one of the ASW Coolfishbags, or even a small thermos flask. You can even go to the lengths of rigging your launce sections on hooks linked to snoods and freeze them down ready to use. That way you only use as many as fishing conditions allow. Any not used can be taken home in a thermos flask and refrozen.

I have heard of fillets of launce being used for bass, but quite honestly, if you have to take a side fillet off one of these, you might as well use a small sandeel. As regards frozen eels, you can buy ready packaged, blast-frozen sandeels from tackle suppliers. I confess I have little faith in them but over the last couple of years I have seen enough pollock and bass caught on them to admit they are a very good standby. They can be quite small and when thawed out do present a few problems to those anglers wanting to cast them out a long way. Better to whip them to a long shank hook using elasticated thread for distance casting, even using a bait clip to streamline them. I suggest blast-frozen eels are just a standby bait for light casting or float work. Take the time and effort to get hold of some freshly netted or dug sandeels if you can. It really is time well spent if you want to contact a bass.

Shellfish

After the peeler crab and sandeel you can use any one of a number of baits for bass fishing. Although at times deemed a finicky feeder, when conditions are hard even the stately bass will be tempted by anything it can get hold of. In this respect you have a tremendous variety of shellfish to choose from. While all will take the bass at some time or other, I have chosen to place them in some sort of order of popularity.

Razorfish, again not the easiest baits to come by, can be very good for both shore and boat fishing for bass, especially when fished as a cocktail bait in conjunction with something else. One of the best combinations is razorfish tipped with ragworm. The razorfish is a south-coast specialist's bait, much prized by anglers working the Open match circuits. If you can get hold of a lot of them, pile a couple onto a long shank and whip them over with elasticated thread. There are two methods for collecting them: either walk the shoreline after a good storm or dig your own. The former is preferable, but you need to be fairly close to the sea in order to capitalise on the free offerings. The best time for collecting is when there has been a storm around a period of spring tides. This is when the sea goes out to its farthest point and consequently the pounding of the waves dislodges the razorfish which, like sandeels, prefers to lie in the area between low spring and low neap tidal marks.

The churning action of the waves will push the razorfish right up onto the high water mark but you need to collect them as soon as possible before any decay sets in. Razorfish will stay fresh in their shells for a couple of days, but left high and dry they will dehydrate, then decompose. They are still perfectly acceptable to the fish but will smell rather unpleasant for the angler baiting them up. In this stage of decomposition I would restrict them to flounder and dab baits fished close in. Collected the day after a storm they can be frozen down, complete with their shells, or used in the next tide.

If you have problems getting to the sea for a collecting session after

Right: This angler knew exactly where and when the bass were feeding, hooking two at once from a low water Sussex shore mark. You must work fast once the bites start to come as bass only feed for short periods during each tide.

a storm you will have to dig your own. Razorfish are found vertically in the sand and are located by the small hole they leave on the surface. One of the easiest ways to catch them is to walk the low tide line looking for such holes and then to pour some table salt down them. In just over a minute the razor will poke out of the top of the hole and you can grab him. I have heard that the salt makes them think the tide is coming in and so they come out to feed. I'm not convinced myself—I believe they come out because they are irritated by the high concentration of salt. You can also spear razorfish at night when they come to the surface, using a specially made V-shaped fork. Make a mental note of where the tip of the razorfish protruded, so that if it disappears after picking up your vibration you can dig away frantically to get it out. A word of advice here. Get down at least a spit and a half of the fork before you start to dig up as the muscle or foot will be the piece of bait you want to avoid snapping off.

To store razorfish, either freeze them or keep them for a couple of days in damp seaweed or even wet cardboard, stacking them in layers. To remove them from the shell carefully slit along the jointed edge, but use a blunt knife rather than a filleting knife otherwise you might lose a finger. There are two varieties, both reaching up to 7 in. in length and both perfectly acceptable to a bass. I would suggest however, that they are clear water rather than dirty water baits. A final tip if you are freezing some after storm collecting and are unsure how old they are: dip them in pilchard oil, shell and all, then drain off before wrapping individually in newspaper and freezing. This will at least give you some scent when you thaw them out.

There are two types of limpets that are of interest to the angler. Slipper limpets, which make very good baits, and rock limpets which do not. Slipper limpets can be collected at the high water mark after a good storm, much the same as the razorfish. There will be a day or so before these baits, dislodged by the tide, will be dead and washed back out to the fish, so build up a good stock by shelling them using a blunt kitchen knife, rolling them in salt, then papering them down and freezing. They should be as tough as old leather when you thaw them out. You generally need to put 4 or 5 on a wide gape hook to make a big enough bait for a bass, elasticating them down to stop them exploding on the cast. I also dispense with the use of a bait clip, preferring to lob them out 50 or 60 yards to land in the littoral zone where most of the food is washed around.

Rock limpets hardly need salting to toughen them up. Found below the high water mark clinging to rocks, these cone-shaped shellfish have to be removed with a hard, sharp rap at the base of the shell. Fail to hit it hard enough and the limpet merely tightens its suction grip and becomes impossible to remove, short of smashing its shell. Scoop out the meat contents and apply as described for slipper limpets, but be warned, they are not nearly as effective. The slipper limpet has softer meat and exudes more juices than the rock limpet. However, rock limpets can make a bass bait when all else fails.

This youngster was delighted with this bass taken from Eastoke corner at Hayling Island. This is a good mark for fishing with slipper limpets after a storm.

Mussels, clams and cockles are all acceptable to the bass. Of the three, I would choose clams as the best bait. Found anywhere from the low to midwater tide lines they can be kept for a day or two in a bucket of wet seaweed. On no account use fresh water, only seawater, and change it whenever you can. To get the meat out, split the hinge of the shell with a blunt knife, then gently scoop out the contents. Some bass specialists only use the yellow mussel or 'foot' as it is known but I prefer to take the time and trouble to tie the whole shellfish onto a hook with elasticated thread. Again, this is a soft bait, so forget about blasting it to oblivion with a 200-yd cast. Most of the fish will take this bait fished close in.

Mussels must be the next most popular and are by far the best as far as smell is concerned. The meat inside is very soft, which means it must be tied to the hookshank with elastic thread if any of it is to survive a cast. Mussels can be found almost anywhere amongst broken ground. They cling to groynes, pilings, bridge buttresses, jetty and pier bases, and rocks. Easy to collect, they congregate in clumps or 'beds' giving anglers easy pickings. Don't bother trying to freeze them as they tend to break up completely. Use them as soon after collecting as possible, leaving them in a bucket of wet seaweed,

The pleasures of fishing the open surf beach are two fold; not only is there the chance of taking a good bass but also the likelihood of a fine quality flounder if you fish lugworm or peeler crab baits. Here Paul Harris admires his catch.

preferably in a cold garage if you want to use them in a day or two. Open the shells by splitting at the base of the hinge, very carefully. The soft meat inside is easily damaged and you will need the meat from half a dozen shells to make up a big blob of mussel meat. No bait clips, just a careful, steady cast out into deep waters should bring the desired result.

If crabs are about and you are fishing in summer you are going to need to replenish hook-baits pretty frequently. Make sure you collect plenty of mussels and scoop out the contents of a couple of dozen shells, keeping the rest laid out on newspaper to dry them up a bit ready for the next hook-bait. I have no idea how the bass feed on mussels in their natural state as the shells are almost impenetrable. My theory is that the bass are hunting the crabs that occupy the area over and around the mussel beds and are used to the smell of the meat from the mussel bed itself. The crab a good shore bait, but better when fished in close proximity to the shellfish bed, or close to a rocky outcrop, rather than over open sand on a surf beach.

Finally there is the cockle. You simply pick these up from along the low tide mark, shell them as soon as you can, dry them on some newspaper, and put them in a small jar or bait container, shaking some salt over them. You can keep them refrigerated for up to 3 days, or freeze them for later on. They provide a small bait and are more often used by the angler after flatfish, largely neglected as a bass bait. Admittedly more useful as a standby bait, you can thread them up the hookshank and bind with elasticated cotton, or simply use them as a 'tip' bait for sliding over the point of the hook if you are using lugworm or ragworm. One of the most difficult parts about collecting cockles is avoiding eating them yourself. I remember them well when I used to buy them by the pint up near Aldgate East Station in the East End of London for my grandfather. He ate them faster than a bass, so they must taste pretty good. I myself never eat shellfish, as I read too much about the cadmium and heavy metal content retained by a large number of shellfish in polluted areas. Use a number 2 or 1/0 hook, threading as many as 4 or 5 cockles up the hookshank.

There are many other shellfish baits worth trying for bass but I feel these will at least give you something to start with and are all collected from a similar sort of ground.

Go Fishing for Bass

Worms

There are three main types of saltwater worm that are most likely to interest the angler: the lugworm, the ragworm and the white ragworm. Of all these, the lugworm is probably the most popular, not because of its success rate but because of its availability. There are few places where you cannot dig a few lug at low tide. As long as the tide is about one third of the way down from the high water mark, you can find their casts. They live in a U-shaped burrow in the sand, making a hole or depression in the sand where they feed at one end, and a curled heap of sand or 'cast' at the other. You can dig for them in two ways. 'Trenching' is one method and is done when the worm casts are particularly prolific. Simply make a trench against the wind to stop any surface water running in and then dig a trench about 3 ft wide, collecting the lugworm as you go. In summer and early autumn they will only be one spit deep. Once the colder weather starts around November, you will have to start going deeper for them. Should you 'fork' or damage any lugworm, be sure to separate them from the live ones, otherwise they will kill them all. Some anglers discard any

An angler fishes an early flood tide for bass using a whole king ragworm at Hinkley Point power station. Some tremendous shore bass have been landed from this venue and there are many more similar low water rock marks yet to be discovered.

Getting hold of fresh lugworms is of paramount importance to the bass angler. Large lugworms, like those shown here, can be fished whole. Smaller 'blow' lugworms should be grouped together on one hook to make a big bait.

49

broken worms but I sort them out into a different container and use them first.

You can also get them individually when the casts are fewer by digging between the cast and 'blowhole', taking great care not to break the individual worm. The best lugworm is called a yellowtail and is quite a big bait, sufficient to be used on its own for bass. 'Blow' lug are smaller, immature worms that may be threaded three at a time up the hookshank and over the eye in order to make a big bait. Finally there is the black lugworm. This chap lies very deep, often eighteen or twenty inches deep, and requires a special spade and considerable effort if it is to be extracted. They should be squeezed from one end to the other to 'gut' them—this makes them stay tough longer.

With any of the lugworm it is necessary to keep them dry and cool. An increase in temperature is the thing most likely to kill off your hard won stock. For this reason I like to wash all my worms in fresh seawater as soon after digging as possible, rinsing them individually and then wrapping them in a fold of newspaper. The more absorbent the paper the better. Some anglers put all their worms in the centre of the paper and then wrap them, but I find they quickly make the newspaper wet and need changing more often. I prefer to take the trouble to wrap mine individually. Keep them dry and more important, keep them cool. You can freeze black lug and use them as a secondary bait, but the ordinary yellowtail and blow lug are not worth storing. Use them as soon after digging as possible, thereby making use of those body juices. Keep them in wet seaweed or just a little damp sand. If the worms are undamaged you can, should you wish to take the trouble, keep them alive for a long time in an aerated seawater aquarium. This method has been used with great success by cod fishermen, but it's only the seasoned bass specialist who does this regularly.

Ragworm are, in my opinion, the best worms for clear water work. Obviously they do not have the same juices as the lugworm, but they will still outfish the lug on clean beaches. I have no idea why this should be so. The ragworm prefers sand that has a greater grit content and can be dug more easily where there are a few stones about, mostly on the banks of estuaries. They come in two colours depending on the spawning season. If the ragworm is green and soft it will be full of eggs and distinctly 'milky', liable to burst on hooking. They will catch fish but tend to be a lot softer for casting. If they are a rusty red they are in prime condition and can be kept for longer periods. There is little point in freezing them unless you want a mushy mess. Once you have dug them, rinse them in fresh seawater and then dry them in newspaper. You can use the dry chips used in loft insulation to keep them in or a bit of silver sand. I prefer the latter which at least retains a little moisture. Kept in a lidless wooden seed tray in very cool sheds or garages, they will last several days. Best of all, put them on the hook just as soon as you can.

It may be worth mentioning that you could be digging up ragworm in brackish estuaries mistaking them for the true red ragworm. These are mostly suited to mullet fishing and are certainly not good for distance casting. They break up easily, so make sure you dig where the ground is firm and gritty, not in the sloppy mud of the estuary.

Finally mention should be made of the white ragworm. This is used primarily by beach matchmen who attach a great deal of importance to its 'wriggleability'! This little chap looks like a standard red rag but is much slimmer, firmer to hold and certainly more active. They are used as a 'tipping' bait when baiting with, for example, razorfish. The idea when using a white rag is to attract visually, their lithe action giving rise to the matchman's nickname, 'snakes'. I therefore see little point in impaling the whole of a white rag onto the shank of a hook. This might make it stay on but it inhibits its one attracting quality, its movement. Far better to hook it through, threading it up the hook about one third of the way from the pincer end, leaving the rest hanging. Long casting would obviously whip the tail off, but used for inshore light tackle fishing in calm seas it is an excellent daytime bass bait. It also works well for floatfishing from shallow rocks for bass.

So, although a sandeel fished live is the number one floatfishing bait, white rag is a close second. That tail wriggling action seems almost irresistible and is excellent for school bass which devour white rag avidly. White rag can be dug while you are working away for either lug or red rag as they seem to inhabit the ground somewhere between the two.

As far as storage is concerned, they are essentially fished as live

A happy fisherman with a fine bass taken from the mouth of a feeder stream that ran onto Cromane Strand in County Cork, Eire. The bait was a blast-frozen Ammo sandeel.

worms, so you must keep them alive. They live well in saltwater aquariums and also fair pretty well in a bucket with an aeration pump. Once one is dead you must immediately remove it from the others, throwing it away rather than freezing it. The white rag is one of those baits best used on a hot summer's day when every other bait has failed.

Fish Baits

The bass is a true predator as can be seen from its large mouth and powerful tail. Although it will take anything, other fish must feature pretty high on the menu. It will attack almost any small fish that can be folded into its mouth and the sandeel, as previously mentioned, is top of the list.

Small mackerel must not be taken too often, for conservation reasons but the number of big bass taken on this bait does encourage the angler to go for mackerel. Bass seem to be attracted to a half mackerel, usually the tail end or even an entire fillet, when ledgered hard on the bottom usually with the intention of catching skate or conger. I have no idea why they take this bait, but they do, so try fishing with a whole baby 6-oz mackerel, affectionately referred to as a 'joey'. Simply hook through the tail and cast out. Alternatively, you can cut off a side fillet of mackerel and try that. My own tip is not to take the standard cuts of mackerel along each flank. Instead, turn the mackerel upside down and take off the entire belly section. Hook just a couple of times through the thinnest point and bind with elasticated cotton. This makes a flashy, silver bait that can flutter about in the tide and tempt that extra finicky fish. I have heard of big double-figure bass being taken on whole mackerel heads intended for conger. I wouldn't advise this method though because it you want a bass, you can end up being pestered by 4-lb strap congers!

A whole baby herring is an effective bait and should you want to fish a strip bait you can take the fillet from anywhere and still keep that bit of flash to your bait. Herrings are best used fresh from the trawler, which again means local anglers will have more chance of getting better bait. They freeze fairly well but try filleting them into several hook-baits first, then rolling them in salt, wrapping each hook-bait individually in cling film and then freezing. That way you can use each bait whenever you want, returning the others to the freezer if unused. Herring is a much better bait than many anglers realise and salting them first helps firm up the meat.

Although bass feed heavily on the sprat shoals once they are in season, I hesitate to advise using them as a hook-bait. Doubtless there will always be an angler about who has landed bass on sprats but I think the use of artificials will produce easier and certainly quicker catches. The same goes for the use of whitebait, which must also form an important part of the bass's diet. Other than groundbaiting with them from piers and jetties, I feel an artificial would work better.

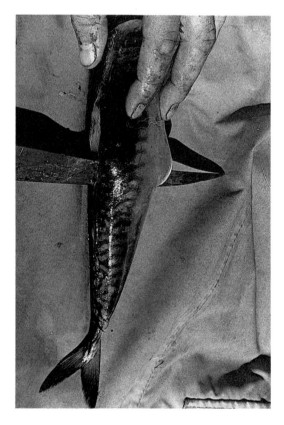

Never be afraid to use a whole fillet taken from the side of a fresh mackerel when fishing for big bass in deep water. Many huge bass have been landed by anglers after conger eels using this bait.

Baits

The humble pouting, a tiny fish, is excellent for big bass, when used in the 4-oz range and fished live. Indeed many big bass used to be caught on freelined pouting fished by anglers around the moorings and dockyards of Portsmouth. These big bass probably spent the entire year around the harbours and jetties, taking advantage of the rich supplies of crustaceans, crabs and tiny fish that lived among the weed covered pilings. At first many of these monster fish were thought to be cruising mullet until one day someone lost a pouting to one and the bass specialists quickly followed suit! The pouting can be used as a deadbait, ledgered on the bottom from boat or shore, but if floatfishing or freelining as a livebait use only the best fish. Hook once through the top lip and allow any taking bass about 5 seconds to get the bait turned head first before you set the hook.

When boat fishing you might come across a species called the poor cod which can resemble a tiny pouting. This little chap is excellent when ledgered dead for conger, but does not keep well as a livebait. Any of these fish used as deadbaits, livebaits or strip baits will, in turn, catch a bass, but I am afraid I cannot tell you which bait will work when and where—that is something to learn for yourself.

Squid and Cuttlefish

There are two types of squid that are of interest to the bass angler, the better of the two being the 'baby' or calamari squid. This is the size most commonly used in restaurants. The other is a large squid, most likely to be found in a fishing trawl and suitable for strip baits. Let's deal with the calamari first. There is no reason for cutting this beautiful bait down any smaller. While it may seem overly large as compared with the worm or crab baits, bigger bass have no hesitation about taking it in a couple of gulps. All you need to do is scale up your hooks a bit more. You can even rig them on a double hook rig, one acting as a retaining hook, inserted near the rounded end of the calamari, the other hidden just near the fringe where the tentacles start. Or you can mount them loosely on a single hook, but remember that when shore fishing there is going to be quite a bit of air resistance and a 60-yd cast is about all you can hope for. For this reason alone I advise using them close to deep water or rock marks, thus putting a big bait near the area a large bass is likely to be patrolling.

You can also use calamari for boat fishing but a long, thin strip of squid meat trailing out from a larger specimen is more likely to be successful. You can double-hook rig this strip, or simply nick the hook through once and leave the rest of it to flutter enticingly in the tide. If using the latter method, remember to allow a few seconds for the bass to get the whole squid strip inside its mouth before setting the hook.

Either type of squid can be purchased from the local wet fishmongers, or possibly your local tackle shop. However, if there is any way you can buy them from a trawler while fresh and freeze them yourself, then do so. They are definitely preferable to older frozen squid. This is also a bait that goes off quickly, especially in the summer heat when you may well be bassing. Try to keep the squid,

Bass do not need gaffing but to avoid a hook pulling out at the last moment when boat fishing, use a net. More bass are lost at the boat due to an excess of enthusiasm than at any other time.

Baits

whether calamari or strips, in a cool box so the meat stays fresh.

The other bait worth mentioning is the cuttlefish. Most of you will be familiar with the 'cuttle' or piece of skeletal bone that finds its way into the budgie's cage. Well, forget about the skeleton and concentrate on getting the meat of a cuttlefish stripped down ready for baits. They really are good and although I cannot imagine the smell is any different to that of the squid, I would class them as better bass catchers. They are difficult to get hold of and the best way is to contact your local trawler skippers, offering them some money to keep you some if they land any. The heads of cuttlefish are fine for bigger species like cod, conger and ling but a little large for bass.

Make sure you wash any ink out of the squid or cuttlefish and peel off any surface skin with a knife. With the spine removed and washed (this has a plastic-like appearance in the squid), you have a first-class bass bait from either of them that is easy to use and very durable. Even crabs have some difficulty getting through this tough meat!

Prawns and Shrimps

Any inshore bass enjoys a stable diet of prawns and shrimps but especially those bass foraging among the weed-covered rocks of shallow pools and creeks where shrimps are prolific. I cannot imagine bass move into this type of ground looking for shrimps alone, but probably come across them in their search for small crabs and fish, nosing among the stones in the sand. Shrimps and larger prawns both make good bass baits but I would stress they are best fished by floatfishing from rocks, where the bait can be drifted into an area of deeper water. I have never had too much success fishing them as a static bait on the bottom and if any crabs are around they will make short work of any shrimp or prawn anchored there.

Bites, when they come, will take the float quickly under the surface so be sure to set the hook before the bass feels the extra drag and ejects the bait. You can also use prawns and shrimps purchased from the fishmongers but don't peel them, fish them whole just nicking the hook once through the tail section. If you get fresh baits, so much the better. The easiest method for gathering them is to wade out around the base of jetties, piers and rocks just prior to low water and sweep a fine mesh shrimping net carefully around the edges. If they are there in any number, you should get plenty without too much effort. The other method is to drop down a circular, fine mesh net, weighted with a piece of lead or iron, tied to a length of rope. This is suitable in deeper water where wading may be impractical due to a soft, muddy bottom or too much water. Tie a couple of pieces of mackerel or a similar disposable fish bait to the mesh, leave it on the bottom for fifteen or twenty minutes, then bring it to the surface rapidly. You should have plenty of hardbacked crabs and hopefully some prawns. Of the two methods, I find netting rock pools and around jetties the best.

One way to avoid crabs getting all your bait is to make a trap from a biscuit tin. Punch a few holes in the tin, put in some offal and lower it to the bottom. It might be worth leaving it there all night. This is a fiddly method but at least you are fairly sure of getting only prawns and not the unwanted by-product, crabs. You can also keep prawns and shrimps alive in an aerated bucket as described previously for sandeels. Care should be exercised when hooking them; use only a fine wire hook, nicking it through a segment near the tail. This allows maximum movement under the float and is far superior to fishing dead prawns. Bass can also be attracted to the floatfished bait by chumming, or groundbaiting, with a mixture of bran, pilchard oil and mashed up shrimps or prawns. This is particularly useful in the quieter areas of water.

Artificial Baits

One of the best ways to take a bass is undoubtedly to capitalise on its instinct to hunt live fish. Apart from fishing with a live pouting around jetties, or floatfishing a live sandeel from rocks, the only other method to catch bass is by using artificial baits. At times, when bass have shoaled up and are harassing a shoal of whitebait or sandeels, they will hit almost any type of artificial bait you care to

Baits

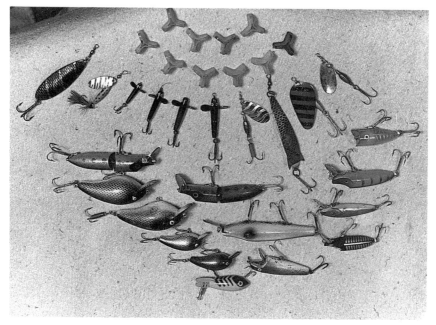

Artificial lure fishing for bass with freshwater plugs is a fairly new trend at the moment yet fishing with a selection of diving lures from rock marks can be highly successful at dawn or dusk.

throw at them. This is particularly true when boat fishing and some of the most incredible hauls of fish have been landed on rod and line using such lures. A few anglers feel this is not a 'sporting' way to catch bass, but until you have thrown a light pirk or spoon at an acre of boiling silver fish it is perhaps unwise to comment. Such frenzied activity seldom lasts long. It may happen at the same time and place each day for 4 or 5 days; it may happen at the same time of day, or state of tide, but further down the coast; or it may happen for 20 minutes every 2 weeks for just 2 months of the year! You certainly cannot just go out and catch them regularly, which is fortunate, otherwise there would be no bass left.

An artificial simulates one of the baitfish being hunted by the bass. The most popular of these must surely be the sandeel. Decades ago sea fishermen, some of them commercial hardliners, made up their own imitation sandeels with sections of rubber tubing, with a cut to

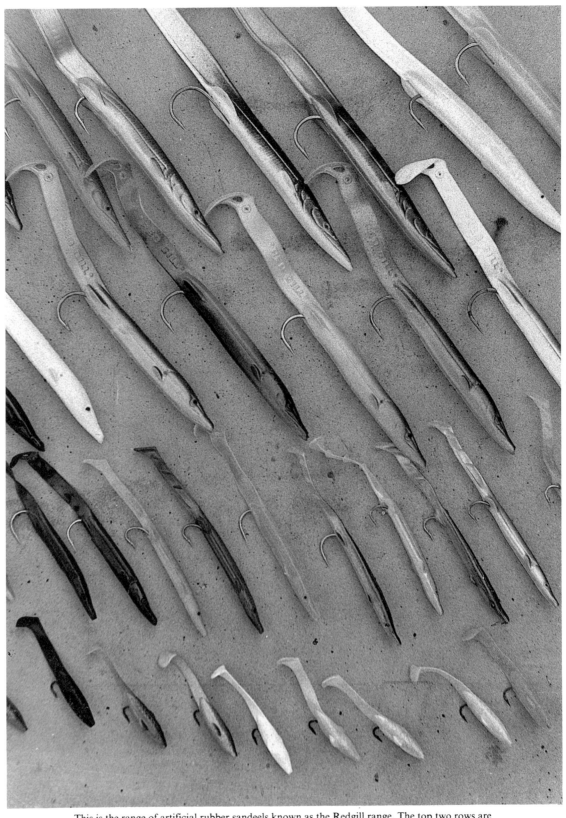

This is the range of artificial rubber sandeels known as the Redgill range. The top two rows are designed for boat fishing, the third row is for shore fishing and the mini Redgills on the lower row are ideal for mackerel and small pollock.

make the tail and a curve in the shank of the hook to make them wiggle when retrieved. They certainly caught their share of fish but of course there were a lot more fish about to catch then anyway. Today you are fishing for fewer fish so you need the very best imitation you can get. This comes in the shape of the Mevagissey based 'Redgill' sandeel, probably the best sea angling lure ever invented. It carries a couple of angled vanes in its tail which gives it a tail-wiggling motion guaranteed to drive the bass wild. They also come in different sizes, which means you can use the small size for light tackle spinning from the shore, or the larger sizes for trolling around reefs in deep water from a boat. You can also troll them slowly behind a moving boat like a natural sandeel.

One of the most controversial methods of taking bass using artificials is pirking. This is a method that I believe may have originated in the north of England where sea fishermen used it to good effect on the cod shoals. Soon it became popular down south and a smaller version of the cod pirk worked very well for bass. It is so simple to make the pirk that many anglers do so at home. All you need is a 4-in. piece of octagonal or hexagonal steel, cut an angled face at either end, drill a couple of holes to take a split ring, then get them chromed. Some people make their own from chrome tubing like cycle handlebars and fill them a third full with lead, flattening either end with a hammer. To the split ring attach a treble hook, to the other, the main line. Now comes the question of sportsmanship. Should such a pirk be fitted with a treble hook or a single hook? The hooking power of a treble is obviously very high and all freshwater pike lures and plugs come factory made with trebles. I see no reason to use a single hook unless your intention is to return every fish you land anyway. Unhooking is certainly easier with a single hook.

There is also the chance to experiment with different colours when pirking and it is easy to dry the metal off with a rag and add some coloured electrical tape such as that made by 3M, in an effort to help make up the bass's mind. Shop bought pirks are available. ABU Egon's are very good and come in a wide variety of sizes. Then there is the Ryobi range of lures called the Solvkroken. They are available in 4 different sizes: the 6 oz, 9 oz, 14 oz and 17 oz. I think you should only use the 6 oz for bassing—manufactured from heavy-gauge,

Go Fishing for Bass

Take advantage of rocky headlands to assess the scene at low tide and discover the best areas to fish. This extra height allows you to see weed, deeper gullies and snaggy areas.

stainless steel metal they can take a lot of punishment. The Rondo slim pirk in 100, 150 and 200 gm weights are also effective. The only pirk I have ever had success with from the shore is the smallest of the ABU Egon range. For most pirking you will need to fish deeper water from a boat.

Shore fishermen often fail to realise that rocky headlands, and indeed any deep water near rocks, provide the ideal terrain for lure fishing. The most successful spoon of its time was the ABU Toby, probably in the 1 oz range. It is still available today. Ryobi market a similar version called Odin lures, again the 1 oz casts well and is available in a variety of bright colours. A popular lure in Ireland was once a long, thin spoon called the German Sprat which was, and still is, used to devastating effect in river entrances where the bass shoal up. The largest catch I have ever heard of using this artificial was a 100-lb catch by one angler on a single tide from County Wexford in southern Ireland.

Baits

This combination of tackle-seat and rucksack, marketed by Normark, is well worth a try. With all your tackle and bait in the main bag and side pockets and the rucksack on your back, your hands are left free for climbing to out of the way rock marks.

The freshwater pike angler's lures offer much untapped sport in terms of lure fishing from the shore. Many are now being shipped over from the United States where lure making has been perfected to a fine art. Possibly one of the best is to use plugs rather than spinners. Lures like the ABU Hi-Lo have an adjustable front vane which you can alter to make the lure run either shallow or deep. This is great when you are fishing a low-water rock mark where the kelp beds hang several feet beneath the surface. Another good lure is the Big-S. This is a floating lure but it dives deeper the faster you retrieve it. For some reason the jointed plugs seem to work better in saltwater and I can only assume their snake-like jiggling action looks similar to that of a big sandeel. Early morning and late evening on a flood tide is about the best time to lure fish as many of the smaller fish rise up out of the weeds and rocks when the light level is lower. Try to avoid the use of 'spinners', a lure with a blade revolving around a bar. They cannot be retrieved fast enough and they mostly pick up mackerel. Lure fishing with the freshwater angler's arsenal opens up a wealth of new possibilities for the shore bass angler—capitalise on them! You can expect a better class of fish when lure fishing near deep water rocks, certainly over the 4-lb mark.

The author uses chest waders to cast into a heavy surf on Garrettstown Strand in Ireland. Bass will often run in the area where the author is standing although in general the bait should be positioned where the waves first start to break.

Take the time to research your marks if the area is new to you. Use an Ordnance Survey map and judge where the wind is likely to blow up a good surf.

Above: Study the water tables when selecting a surf beach to fish bass. As a general rule, on these shallow beaches a lack of waves indicates a lack of fish.

Below: A small, open, sand beach between rocky headlands is ideal for bass fishing with lug or ragworm. Distance is not important but a long, flowing trace is necessary to allow the bait to roll around freely.

This huge bass was taken by Norman Message, a specialist small boat angler, from Eastbourne's Beachy Head. Each year big shoals of bass move in to feed on the shoals of whitebait and sandeels that gather over the rocks and in the tide race.

There is no need to keep every bass you land. This is a very respectable catch and any others should be returned to provide a breeding stock for future years.

The author's wife, Hilary Pullen, gets to grips with a double-figure striped bass taken on anchovy freelined along a canyon wall on Lake Powell, Utah, U.S.A.

Above left: The author grabs an 8-lb striped bass hooked in the splendour of the Grand Canyon where he fishes successfully without a guide.

Above right: A superb catch of freshwater striped bass. The author runs the boat with his wife and has fished in both Arizona and Utah for striped bass, locating the fish without any sophisticated fish-finding equipment but relying solely on his experience of reading water conditions.

Right: The striped bass is a great predator and can be taken on jigs as well as baits and standard lures. Our own European bass also has a high tolerance of freshwater, often venturing far inland in rivers.

The solitude of the bass fisherman; the Strand at Brandon Bay, County Kerry.

Tackle

Choosing the correct tackle is always of paramount importance to the bass angler, particularly if he intends to pursue the species from the shore. Obviously you can take bass on a wide range of heavier rods and reels but if a degree of sport is to be retained, then you should look at the best range of tackle that is going to be some pleasure to use.

Rods

Boat rods are fairly simple. For this range of fishing you need not worry about heavy wrecking rods but go for something more 'tippy' like the uptiding rods even though you may not be using them for this specialised purpose. Ryobi market a handy range called the System 5. This is a revolutionary new concept in boat rod designs in as much as you get three different weight tips coupled to two different butts. They are sensitive in the tip section for bite registration and have duplon hand grips that don't twist, screw reel fittings and ceramic lined guides to resist friction wear. This provides a selection of rod tops suitable for all types of bait fishing, whether you're anchored or drifting over a sandbank or feeling the rod tip pull slowly as a bass sucks in that artificial sandeel. For pirking from the boat you need something with a little more beef, not to boat the fish but to make the pirk work properly in a sweeping, upward motion. You need something like the Beastmaster rods from Shimano. I have a one piece 20/50-lb class blank that has a tip sensitive enough to detect takes yet power enough to sweep a 12-oz pirk off the bottom if required. These rods are built for quality and are ideal for the serious angler who wants to invest money in a rod that is unlikely ever to let him down. These two makes of rods cover all your requirements when boat fishing for bass.

Fishing from the shore is a different matter. You will be aiming to throw either a lure or a bait way out beyond the waves and will be guided by conditions and necessary technique rather than simply requiring a tool to drag the fish in with. Hooking the fish should be your first and foremost priority. For spinning lures such as Toby or Odins from the rocks you can actually make do with a Ryobi Masterpike 2 freshwater rod. This rod handles line strengths from 8

Professional shore guide Ed Schliffke climbed down the treacherous rocks of Trevose Head in Devon to carry up one of the author's bass. Ed provides such a good service that he will not allow his clients to go down the rocks to bring up fish.

to 12 lb and can incorporate butts for either fixed spool or multiplier casting. Reaching 9 ft in length when fitted up, you can whip a lure out a fair old distance and put a healthy bend in the rod when you hit even a modest bass.

When surfcasting however, you will have a long way to go in order to better the new Super Bass marketed by Conoflex. This is a specification-design bass rod intended to throw a mere 3-oz lead well out whilst retaining tip sensitivity when you get a hookup. A carbon/kevlar construction, its aim is to enable the bass angler wading in the surf to hold the rod all the time without getting aching arms. The blank can be ordered from most tackle shops and you can then build it yourself or get the shop to build it up for you. There are 2 versions available: a 7-ft tip with a 6-ft butt, or a 7-ft tip with a 5-ft butt. There is a glass tip in the blank that gives you that extra sensitivity, allowing you to feel a taking fish before it feels you. This rod fills the bill nicely but if you want a step up for rough sea fishing when you need a 5-oz lead, try the Conoflex 2600. This is a standard-style beachcaster that can be used for both standard and pendulum casting.

Reels

With regard to reels, you could spend a lot of money and time and still be no better off. When boat fishing for the average sized bass, use the Ryobi S320 multiplier. Cheap and cheerful, this has a star drag perfectly adequate for subduing most bass. It also casts fairly well if you take out the manufacturer's grease and replace it with light oil so it can be used for both downtide and uptide techniques. There are suitable sizes for both 12-lb and 20-lb line classes and they can also be purchased with a levelwind attachment. This covers the cheaper end of the market, but should you be pirking with a Beastmaster rod or generally aiming for a higher than average bass, you may want the luxury of a lever drag reel. Here you have the advantage of the very latest in technology for Shimano now offer a wide range of competitively priced Triton lever drags, from the tiny TLD-5 to the TLD-25. You can use any line range from 6 lb right up to 30 lb and be sure that those titanium drag plates will only give line steadily under pressure. They are fitted with 4 ball bearings; a one-piece frame that will not distort under pressure. Looked after correctly, they should provide service for years.

If you are a beginner or want something easy to use, try a fixed-spool reel. This is cheap to buy, easy to cast with and just as capable of landing big bass as the most expensive multiplier.

Tackle

When beach fishing you have to think primarily of a fixed spool reel for your spinning requirements. This is due to the difficulty in casting very light spinners, spoons and plugs when using a multiplier. I find it far easier to use a fixed spool. All the models in the tackle shops will work but again, the very best will last longer. Go for any of the Shimano Carbomatic range which features the stern drag and pre-set drag facility. This is ideal for shore spinning as besides having a high gear retrieve ratio, the pre-set drag facility means you can set it tight for casting and striking, yet still give line to a taking fish under pressure. You can easily move the drag lever and still return it to the original setting without fear of line breakage.

For the Super Bass beach or surf rod you have a choice of two multipliers. The Ryobi T2 is a new design reel that holds up to 140 yds of 12-lb test in the T1 model or over 270 yds of 12-lb test in the T2 model. I prefer the T2, which can also be converted to suit the ambidextrous. It has a handle drag instead of a star or lever drag and the setting is changed by depressing a button and turning the handle. With a level wind, a magnetic braking option and a lightning-engage

The multiplier is a fine tool for casting from the open surf beaches but it can be difficult to master. This Ryobi T2 has magnetic brakes to assist beginners with spool speeds on the cast.

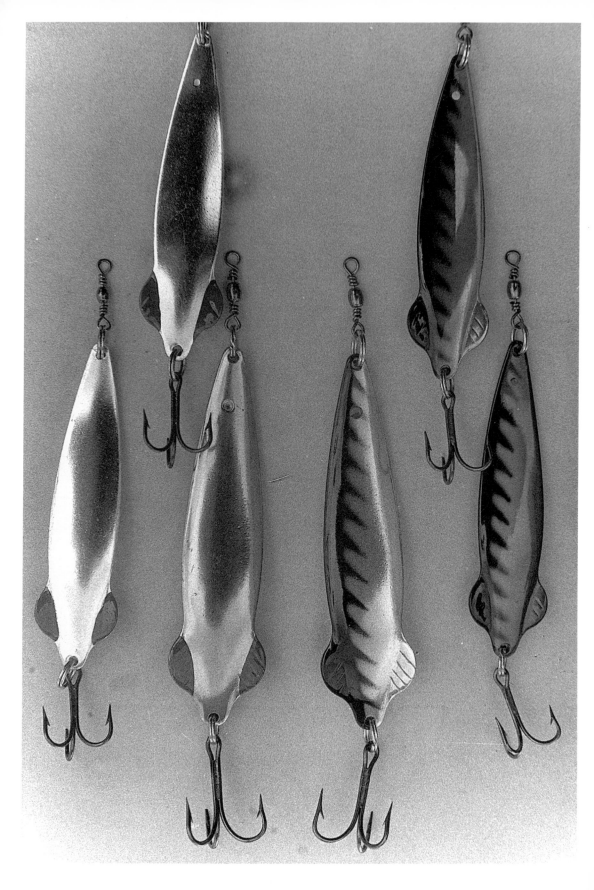

trip bar it performs very well and even feels right on the Super Bass blank. If you want a reel with more power and the ability to throw the bait a long way, go for the Shimano Speedmaster. This reel has taken the beach scene by storm with its fighting drag option, its wrap around spool frame for pendulum casting and its 3 ball bearing races for smooth casting. Nominated as the reel of 1988, I have now landed quite a few fish using it and have certainly had a lot of luck shore bassing with it. It features a fantastic 6.1:1 gear retrieve ratio, a factor which enables you to clear tackle from a snag-ridden bass haunt quickly. A graphite body construction ensures there is no corrosion and it features the same titanium drag surfaces as the Triton TLD series.

Lines

For boat fishing, I see no reason for sticking to medium-heavy weight lines like those guaranteeing a 30-lb breaking point. Tidal conditions will obviously dictate lines to a certain degree but as you are after a species of fish that is unlikely to run into double figures, use 12 or 15 lb. If you are shore fishing there is no reason to rise above 15-lb main line and you can even fish with 12 lb on a multiplier or fixed spool provided you use a shock leader. This is a length of line, about 20 ft long, that should be tied to the end of your reel line before you tie on your terminal rig. It should be at least a 30-lb line, progressing up to 50 lb if you intend using a pendulum cast. While you can use any make of line for this, the American company DuPont market a gold-coloured line called Stren. This is very soft, has a good knot strength and is highly visible to aid casting in low light conditions. A lot of anglers use this make for 'shockers'.

When spinning from rocks or floatfishing with lighter tackle, the corresponding line need only be about an 8-lb line. Anything heavier on the smaller size reel will inhibit casting distance. The further you cast that lure or float, the more likely you are to hit a fish. I nearly

Left: The new long lures in the Odin tackle range (by Ryobi) give the bass fisherman an excellent selection of artificials for casting from the rocks or open beach.

Go Fishing for Bass

always use just one line now, Ande, made in Florida, USA. For about 30 years, Ande has provided top quality, monofilament fishing lines and presently holds over 400 world line-class records. There are 3 major Ande lines: Premium, Tournament and Super Soft, ranging from 2-lb right up to 400-lb test. You can buy the lines in bulk spools and it may be worth importing them direct from Ande, sharing the cost between a group of you. When a spool of line extends several thousands of yards, you can afford to refill the beach reels every time you mess up the line with an overrun. While Ande hit the spot for all ranges of fishing, I feel I should mention one of the cheaper makes. Ande is top quality and if you are a beginner you may not want to lay out cash for a bulk spool. Try the Ryobi range of the Red Boat Mono in 12, 15 and 20-lb test ranges or the Green Shore Mono in 12, 15 and 18-lb test ranges. The Masterline Marine Mono is strong with medium stretch and all varieties are available on 330-yd 'one-fill' spools.

Leads

As far as leads are concerned, use the leads which best suit your conditions. For beachcasting from the shore you need a selection of both grip leads and plain bombs in the following 4 sizes only: 3 oz, 4 oz, 5 oz and 6 oz. There is no need for anything heavier because if you cannot hold bottom in the surf with a 6-oz bomb, you certainly should do so with a 4-oz grip lead. The grip leads can be made with collapsible wires and I would advise you to make all your own lead requirements. My own lead requirements are easily catered for as I am lucky enough to have an uncle who owns one of the biggest tyre distribution centres in the south of England. With wheel balancing going on every day, I can get hold of as many lead cast offs as I need!

The best range of lead-making moulds comes from DCA moulds in Wales. They have been supplying tackle shops for years and ranges include many different shapes for both boat and shore. You can get the moulds pre-drilled to enable you to position your wires for the grip leads, then use either beads and wire pressure to hold the arms in position or an elastic band. I use the band method because I'm too tight to splash out on beads!

When boat fishing, you only need 4- and 6-oz grip-wire leads if you are uptiding. For other occasions go for the Aquapedo 4-oz shape from, say, 2-oz up to 1 lb. Beyond that there's no sport in the fishing. The fun of bass fishing is getting plenty of sport on light tackle, not hauling them in on 50-lb shark outfits. Before making leads yourself, write to DCA moulds using the address on their packaging and ask them for the correct procedure to avoid any mishaps. It is vital to keep away from any source of moisture when making leads. If molten lead comes into contact with water it can explode in your face, so take the proper precautions.

The author had some competition when he fished the famous Inch Strand in Ireland for surf bass. Using a camera hidden inside his bag and a remote control shutter release, he captured these amazing sequence pictures (see page 82) of a vixen stealing one of his $3^1/_2$-lb bass to feed her cubs. She also departed with a 1-lb flounder and a whole currant cake!

Tackle

Hooks

Each angler has his own favourite hooks and you will probably want
to try several before you find the best for you, but whatever you use,
make sure the hook point is sharp. This is particularly important
when surf fishing and the bass are running the shallow tables of water
looking for food. You get a crashing bite but if that hook point fails
to penetrate then you have missed your chance.

My first choice is the John Holden range of sea hooks from
Partridge of Redditch. The Managing Director, Alan Bramley, has
given me plenty of different patterns to try, in fact too many at times,
but I finally had success with the John Holden range in sizes 1/0 up to
6/0. This covers every bait eventuality from a live sandeel to a tiny
lugworm, or even a large peeler crab. Their only failing, if it is one, is
that the wire is a fraction too light for my liking. When worm fishing,
that springy effect in the smaller sizes has caused a few bass to
'spring' the hook open and escape. The hook springs back into shape
and some anglers may never realise they lost a fish but when out in
the clear water surf with a pair of chest waders on you can actually
see the fish. The only consolation for me is that I would probably
have returned it alive anyway! The other leading hook makers are
Mustad and they offer thicker wire hooks in hundreds of patterns
and sizes. Take my advice and try Partridge first, then look through
the rest of the market. Keep a lookout for chemically sharpened
hooks—they are excellent.

Techniques

Whether you are fishing for bass from the shore or from a boat, a variety of different techniques surround both methods. Boat fishing may involve surface trolling, casting, pirking, downtiding or uptiding; shore fishing may encompass floatfishing, spinning, surf fishing or rock fishing.

Boat Fishing

Let us start with boat fishing, remembering that location is half the battle in catching any fish. One of the oldest methods used primarily in the clear waters of Devon and Cornwall, is trolling. Years ago it was called 'whiffing' and involved slowly motoring a dinghy along at maybe 2 or 3 knots, trailing a rubber eel a long distance behind the boat. Often at least 60 yds of line had to be let out to make the eel run just below the surface, with a swivel tied into the trace about 12 ft up from the hook. I used this method regularly with the commercial crabbers in Looe, Cornwall, when they used to take out early morning or evening trips in between pulling the pots. They had a regular trolling area around Looe Island and took many fine catches from there. The take when it comes is quite savage but you must resist the urge to strike, letting the motion of the boat pull the hook into the bass's jaw. This method is rarely used now but it is still highly effective where there is a concentrated area of bass, even if only for a limited period.

Few anglers get the chance to see a bag of bass like this. Bob Edwards (left) and Norman Message took this catch on artificial sandeels fished over a rock mark off Eastbourne.

Go Fishing for Bass

'Driftlining' was a variation on the slow trolling technique and was carried out in the famous bass areas like Teignmouth, Salcombe and Padstow. Live sandeels were freelined away from an anchored boat using the tide. The fuller spring tides were better for this method. Years ago, pier anglers also found freelining successful and they specialised in catching the bigger bass living around the ironwork. They lowered a whole squid down in the tide to wash around the pier pilings—and usually hooked a lot of very big bass.

'Whiffing' or surface trolling enables the boat to move into quite shallow bays and areas around headlands. Should you need to make a sharp turn in the boat, wind in the lines and reset them rather than run the risk of dragging a tangle of monofilament along for the next half hour.

A method that might well prove productive is deep slow trolling with the use of downriggers. In America, South Africa, Kenya and other countries, downrigger weights to take the lure down to a predetermined depth are used all the time. Here in Britain their use is still very limited. Many shoals of bass take up residence in water over 40 ft deep, often around rocky outcrops. They do not respond to pirking and are too deep to see a surface-trolled eel. By running a sandeel down on a downrigger system you can pull the lure laterally through the water at the level at which the fish are lying. The use of this method may well catch some of our yet undiscovered bass shoals.

Drifting is standard practice when boat fishing sandeels. It is best in shallow water near sandbars where any engine noise may spook the fish. You can use freeline tactics if the wind and tide are slack, or just enough lead to bounce the bottom, dragging the eel or cut bait along the sand. A live sandeel is the best bait for this type of fishing and the rod should be held all the time, with the line held over the index finger to feel any take. When it comes, make sure you pause a second or two, allowing the bass to hold the eel in its mouth and move off. The pause will be worth it. The second best bait for drifting is a dead sandeel; failing that, a fillet from the side of a launce or greater sandeel does well or, if nothing else, a belly strip of mackerel. A whole baby squid mounted on a double-hook rig is useful for bass over 5 lb. I have had no success using worms when drifting—they seem better when concentrated in one spot. This may well be due to the fact that the scent trail given off by their body juices is too slight to spread very far.

For drifting the deep water rock marks, fish a long flowing trace and several ounces of lead, retrieving slowly in the lower third of the water's depth. This is my favourite method of taking bass, particularly on very light tackle. Large spring tides make the fish more active and enable you to use a lighter lead to get the line angled well away from the boat. You do not want the line to run straight down. In contrast, the use of small pirks requires a slower drift and the results are certainly better with the line straight up and down. Drop the pirk to the bottom, quickly put the reel in gear, remembering you may be over snaggy rock, and pump the rod tip up in a steady sweeping movement. There is no need for violent snatching, just a steady lifting motion. The pirk flutters to the bottom, then rises sharply about 4 ft up. This is the best method for taking a number of bass when they are hard on the feed and some anglers fish small pirks on the bottom of a set of flasher feathers, or even fish a single redgill artificial sandeel about 3 ft up from the pirk on a short flowing trace. Both catch numbers of fish but personally I feel the best bassing involves catching the fishing individually.

Bass invariably feed heavily on sandeel or whitebait shoals, close to, or at the back of, any tide race. Whether it is easier for them to catch the bait in such fast water I don't know. Depending on wind and tidal conditions, there will also be a time, usually only a few days in each year, when the bass actually have the whitebait shoaling on the surface in a blind panic. The bass themselves boil on the surface, chasing the tiny fish, and it is then that you can catch them by casting. You need only a light spinning rod, as described for shore spinning, and a Toby or Odin lure. In fact, when the bass shoal hard enough they will hit virtually anything that lands in front of them. They can also be landed using trout flyfishing tackle under these conditions but this is merely a different rather than a better way of taking them.

Now let us consider bait fishing from an anchored boat. This is going to be the usual way of fishing on the majority of charter boats and it involves 2 techniques: uptiding and downtiding. The latter is standard practice, while uptiding is still fairly new and many old-time

Go Fishing for Bass

This incredible catch confirms the author's belief that artificial sandeels produce good results when boat fishing for bass. In October 1988, Eastbourne anglers Norman Message and Bob Edwards made a huge catch of bass on Redgill eels. Every fish weighed over 8 lb, the largest weighing 10 lb 4 oz, 10 lb 10 oz and 10 lb 14 oz. A once in a lifetime catch!

skippers still find it difficult to accept. You will have to take my advice and believe that it does indeed work. Uptiding developed on the south east coast of England where trips were made to the offshore sandbanks in pursuit of cod, bass and tope. It was thought that the very fast tides, forcing their pressure along the anchor rope and around the boat hull, put off any fish coming near the baits. It is difficult to disprove this theory but I think in general the wider spread of baits sends out a wider spread of scent trails, thus giving the fish something to home in on.

For uptiding, you need to rig up a running ledger but substitute the plain bomb with a break-out grip lead with collapsible wires. When bass fishing you still need a long flowing trace and to overcome problems of casting in a confined area you simply drop the hook bend onto one of the wires of the casting weights. As it hits the water it is knocked free and floats freely downtide. When a fish takes a small bait it often bangs up against the pull of the grip lead, nicking the hook into its jaw a bit, which aids hooking. If the tide is really strong you will need to let out quite a quantity of line so that the pressure of the tide pulls the grip wires into the sand, rather than pulling them across it. You need a longer rod, possibly up to 8 or 9 ft, for this sort of casting and of course with the lines spaced out more, you should have less tangles. If you are fishing independently on a charter boat booked by others, always ask their permission before you uptide. Despite the growing popularity and increased fish catches, some people are still a bit wary of it.

Downtiding simply entails slowly lowering the lead over the side of the boat, letting the lead hit the bottom, then staying in contact with the lead to ensure your bait is in the right place. Although bass are predatory, rising to whatever depth their food reaches, you will find more fish if you keep the bait down near the bottom. With slack or neap tides there will be no water movement to put pressure on the line. In areas where the tide run is hard however, or on a big spring tide, the line may be thrown up with water pressure and the bait lifted off the bottom to hang several yards above the fish's head! Keep adjusting the length of line you have out by raising the rod top quickly, letting the line free spool until you feel the lead hit the bottom, then re-engaging the reel. You can do this until the line is slanted well away from the boat and the water pressure runs down the line, rather than pushing against it vertically. This is called bouncing the bait back. The larger the bait, the more time you should give the bass to take it. There is no way you are going to know what size fish is mouthing the bait and striking too soon just spooks them. I find they rarely come back for a second go.

Shore Fishing

When shore fishing, your main aim is to put your bait in the area you believe the fish are feeding in. At sea, aboard a boat, the bass can be anywhere, and you are dependent entirely on the skipper's judgement, and his experience at reading the echo sounder, to put you in touch with the fish. This is the main reason why I feel a bass caught from the shore is worth half a dozen caught from a boat.

Let's deal with the light tackle aspect first—floatfishing and light spinning. When using a float you may be restricting yourself to 3 distinctly different baits. The best, a live sandeel, may stay alive all day if lightly hooked and undamaged, although we're hoping a big bass will eat it first cast! Your float, held at a predetermined depth with a bead and stop knot, dances in the waves. If you are watching carefully, you may see it tugged down sharply once as the bass grabs the live eel. Whatever you do, do not strike. Watch the float to see if it stays underwater as the bass turns the sandeel, folding it into its mouth. If the float stays under for 2 or 3 seconds then set the hook—you do not want to alert the bass by allowing it to feel the drag from the float. If you use the second bait, one or two prawns, you need to strike almost as soon as the float pulls away, otherwise

This angler is well in with a chance. A gentle surf starting to form, a sinking sun and a flood tide to bring in those foraging bass. He should have a fish on the beach by nightfall.

the bass crunches up the prawns and spits them out, just leaving you with a piece of shell hanging on the hook. The same goes for shrimps, whether you fish them live or dead. The third bait you might try is a belly strip of mackerel. If it is cut very thinly, I feel sure the bass will take it because it looks like a sandeel, maybe even a launce. Again, you should allow 2 or 3 seconds before setting the hook. As far as depth is concerned, I would fish live sandeels and live prawns in the top half of the water's depth and dead sandeels or a belly strip of mackerel in the lower half, letting it trail along the bottom where possible.

When spinning, you can either wade out if you are fishing a surf beach and cast straight out or, if the water is exceptionally clear, work the spoons through the water tables parallel to the shore. Very often bass run the length of a beach, staying in one particular depth of water, hunting into the flow of the tide. Small redgills are ineffective at this depth but with a spoon you can hold the rod top high and allow it to flutter down to the sand, then start it off again. When rock fishing—rocks adjacent to a beach are excellent—cast out across the direction of the waves and allow time for the lure to sink. Rather than continually retrieving the spoon at a standard rate, you may do better to pump the rod hard, without winding, and then let the spoon flutter backwards before taking up the slack. Often the bass will hit the lure as it flutters back but you also miss a few doing this as the trebles are masked by the spoon itself.

Another area to lure fish is around the mouth of a river where it runs off the beach into the sea or at the entrance to an estuary. Here, at the flood and ebb states of the tide, small fish and eels will be washed around, concentrated in the fast flow. The bass capitalise on this and can be taken by casting into the fastest area of flow, letting the spoon toss around in the current. Takes can be savage, so be sure to set the reel's drag. Lure fishing can be a great way of taking bass simply because it means you can rove around carrying the bare requirements for fishing—a rod, a bag, a box of lures and maybe a wooden or metal priest for whacking the fish on the head should you wish to keep it. Most of the time I hope you will release bass to ensure at least some chance of a future sport. Spoons are certainly most successful when used on and around surf beaches and in estuaries and freshwater streams but the freshwater plug is better off rocks.

Low tide seems best for plug fishing, and I have been assured by plug fishing enthusiasts that this is due to the fish being confined to a smaller area of water. With heavily-weeded low water marks however, tackle losses can be extensive. A good freshwater plug costs at least £3, so you don't want to lose too many. I would have thought it advisable to fish the first of the flood, when the smaller fish, living amongst the kelp and weeds, gain confidence with the fresh turn of the sea and rise up out of the shallow water to feed a bit higher up. Once they leave the top fringe of weeds they must surely be the object of attention for any passing bass? This is only my theory but it may well be true as I have always found an early flood good for most species, especially when the light is dull due to low cloud or the approach of evening.

You would think bass need plenty of light to see the baitfish better but this is not so. In fact failing light sometimes sends them on a feeding spree for an hour or more. In these conditions, I suggest you fish a slow diving plug over the top of any weeds at very low water, then bring it up higher or change to a shallower diving model as the flood puts more depth over the weeds. When fishing from very sheer cliffs into deep water the same does not apply as there is always a good depth of water over the weeds. In these situations, you may even have to add some weight uptrace from the lure to help get it down. The traditional crescent-shaped lead, a Wye lead, comes, I believe, from the armoury of the salmon spinner in larger rivers. They too need to get the bait and lure down in the fast current to reach the fish. On jetties, piers and in sheltered coves, you may find the high water period gives you the most strikes. The steadily rising depth of water covers a broken terrain of boulders and small rocks, the sort of country where a foraging bass might well lurk.

There is nothing really new about artificial lure fishing for bass but few anglers are prepared to experiment with it. It is certainly a method of the future with so many modern American lures now being imported, all of which have something different to offer. Inshore bass stocks may have taken something of a hammering from the commercial netters, but one of the few places they cannot net them is in the snaggy, rock-ridden waters close to the shore. It may

Techniques

If you hook a bass over these boulder-strewn beaches you have to crank like crazy to keep the lead from snagging. As you quickly pump and wind, try to lay the line evenly on the spool; this should give you a trouble-free cast next throw.

well be that the only decent-sized bass stocks available to the shore angler in the future will be in these areas. Learning the art of lure fishing is therefore proving increasingly necessary.

Beach Casting

There are several techniques for fishing from beaches but first let's look at surf fishing. In Ireland, Cornwall and Wales there are plenty of 'true' surf beaches—long, crescent-shaped beaches washed clean by the remorseless scouring action of the tide. They are generally fine sand beaches, but occasionally fine shingle, much favoured by the sandeel as a habitat. With no wind these beaches remain flat and featureless, the fishing virtually useless. The exception may be night fishing for flatfish. When the wind blows on or slightly at an angle to the beach, the surf starts to pound, stirring up the sand into clouds, and releasing food particles into the water. Small fish and sandeels move into this area to feed, closely followed by their predators.

Although a good wind encourages the waves to produce a surf, conditions may still not be ideal. Any wave action is good but with an off-shore wind the waves will merely be rolling, rather than surging, in. In order to understand this further you should know how a wave surfs. A wave is formed by wind pushing it along the sea; it rises and falls, then as it comes into contact with shallower waters, it meets the resistance of the seabed. The bottom of the wave moves more slowly than the top and in effect, it trips over itself. The white cap forms, it tumbles over and foams. But when you have a surf produced by a swell in the ocean, either before or after a good storm, then you get a body of water moving into the beach even with very little wind. When the wind is blowing, the same 'trip-up' principle applies as before but this time there is the swell of the sea to push the wave creaming up the surf beach for dozens of yards. This in turn leaves water tables at different depths between each wave break. The waves may be coming in and surfing up to 4 or 5 breakers deep. This is true surf and these

Right: Conditions couldn't be worse for this bass angler. A flat sea, a virtually cloudless sky and a falling tide. Better to wait until there is a flood tide at dusk, even if there is no surf.

are the ideal conditions for bass. They will run the length of the water tables, parallel to the beach in their quest for prey.

There used to be a theory that you needed at least 3 breakers all surfing at once to get the bass running and that you needed to cast to the third breaker. It is possible to cast too far, especially with modern rods like Conoflex 2600 and Super Bass 3 oz. The fish will be in the backwash area where the waves are clearer but still have a hint of colour from suspended sand particles. I have caught bass at 120 yards, well out in the clear water, and even 30 yards out in the creaming white surf. It all depends on the wave pattern, the strength of the wind, the depth and distance between the water tables, and the power of the tide. It is also worth remembering that a storm or strong wind on a flooding spring tide that is rising will help lift up all the rubbish and weed deposited at the previous high water mark. You will then have a lot of rubbish to contend with on the following tide. If there is too much of a stir up the bass do not come in at all.

Having established that the surf in front of you is fishable, you have two choices: either to fish a grip lead or let a bomb lead roll your bait around. While I like a rolling bait or at least a lightly anchored lead best, there are occasions when a fixed grip lead is more successful. If you are using a small bait like a single lugworm, you may find a bass will take it, move off and, feeling the lead, drop it again. It may happen rarely but it is not unknown. When using a grip lead the bass runs the water tables, spots or smells the worm, picks it up and moving off, comes into contact with the fixed lead. With a big bass of 5 lb or more, the force with which the fish hits the lead can give the angler a rod-jolting experience and even cause the grip wires on the lead to open out. If this happens you get slack line all around your feet, so wind like mad to catch up with the fish. If you are up to your armpits in chest waders, try walking steadily backwards, winding fast to keep contact with the bass.

If you are using a larger bait such as a fillet of mackerel, a whole launce or an edible peeler crab, then the grip lead can be a positive disadvantage. A bass holds a big bait for quite a while trying to swallow it and if it feels any resistance from the lead, it drops the bait and spooks. Here you need to use a plain bomb that can almost be carried around in the tide or surf. The bass takes the bait, alerting the angler with a slight knock at the top of the rod and bumping the lead a fraction. I like to slightly bend my rod top, so that if a bite comes again, I can lower the rod top, and should a further bite come, I can let out some slack line, just for a moment or two, before I set the hook. Even so, you are still going to miss a fair number of fish on big baits. You can change from the fixed paternoster, so popular with the grip lead experts, and use a running ledger but you will almost certainly need to clip a big bait down prior to casting. It's not so much the extra distance you are after as the avoidance of damaged bait. You do not want a misaligned hook that might turn back in on the bait on striking and result in a missed fish. When using whole sides of mackerel, big edible peelers or a squid head, pull them into shape with the thread and ensure that the hook point is standing away from the side of the bait at 90°. You should try fishing at different distances if bites are not coming too quickly. Very often bass running a surf strand will travel up and down at a particular table depth. Finding that feeding depth presents the biggest problem in catching them.

As for fishing steep shingle beaches, the situation can still be very hit and miss. The bass will come through at a particular state of the tide, probably very close to shore. The littoral zone will extend only 30 yards out, sometimes less, and the scouring action of the wave on the bottom diminishes quicker the deeper the water. I therefore suggest you fish a big squid or mackerel head bait only 30 or 40 yards out, on a rolling, running ledger rig. The best of the fishing will be on a high water spring in the evening darkness; try to fish a couple of rods if possible. I advocate the use of big baits because the bass will be large, unlike the 2 pounders you catch on the shallow surf beaches. If you do hook one it is quite likely to weigh over 5 lb, although you should not expect to get more than the one fish. There is no point in using a single lugworm, as you will only attract the attention of unwanted fringe species like dabs, pout or whiting. Steep shingle beaches can hold some excellent bass, and while a good steady wave action gives the best of the fishing, there may be occasions, perhaps only 3 or 4 times a year, when the bass will shoal together to chase mackerel and whitebait on the surface. Years ago this would happen more regularly but today, with far less bass in our waters, they only

Go Fishing for Bass

push baitfish to the surface on flat, calm, summer dawns or July evenings. Then it may be possible to take them by spinning, using the technique described for surf spinning.

Rock Fishing

Finally we should turn our attention to rock fishing for bass. Again, you are not going to haul them out three at a time. You should be after just one good fish and given good conditions and a little luck, you could walk up the rocks with an 8-lb bass under your arm. Down at Portland Bill in Dorset, a breed of anglers specialise in rock fishing at night for some of the immense conger that inhabit the waters. They have landed fish of over 50 lb using very large mackerel baits. At certain times of the year they also hit big bass—up into double figures—on baits intended for conger. Portland Bill cannot be the only place where this happens. Big bass are solitary creatures and will work the same territory for as long as the food supply lasts. I believe they may not venture more than a few miles over an entire season and tagging statistics have confirmed that most bass stay within a fairly well-defined area.

The best time for rock fishing will be at night but try to fish in pairs or a group and take along a rope for safety purposes. On one rock fishing session in the Isles of Scilly, one of our party packed up at about 1 am, said goodbye, and was then discovered an hour later, trapped after a fall down a crevice, all his tackle and terminal gear lost for good. If the tide had been flooding and conditions rough, he may well have died. It is not worth fishing dangerous rocks or areas that are going to continually result in you losing gear. You need to be able to reach a patch of clean, sandy ground or shingle fairly close to the rocks. The bass will be hunting the fringes of the rough ground and you want to position your bait out on the sand, but not too far out. I am afraid there is no easy way of defining the clean areas. Unless you are fortunate enough to get hold of local information on where the clean ground is, you have to expect tackle losses, continually casting around until you start to get your gear back. The approach is the same for fishing deep water rock marks.

Techniques

Great care should be exercised when climbing down to some of the more obscure rock marks. Pass the rods down to each other and take your time, especially in rough conditions or after rain. Studded waders must not be worn.

Techniques

For shallow, rough ground that may have small rocks, boulders and patchy areas of clean ground, I advise using peeler crabs as bait. Here you will have to be quite specific about placing the bait, and I suggest a low water recce to check out where everything is. The best time to do this is on a low water spring tide, preferably when there is no wind. The water will then be at its lowest and clearest allowing you to see the dark shadows of the kelp beds. In coloured water areas like the Bristol Channel you can have problems. One answer is to take a rod along, attach a single hook and an old bolt and tie it to a weak link of 10-lb line. Cast out and bump the bolt back over the bottom until you find the snags. If you are finding snags at very low water with a 40 to 50-yd cast, there is little point in fishing the water as the further the flood tide pushes you back up the shore, the more chance you have of losing your gear. At night things get even worse.

The bass move into gullies and clear patches with a flooding tide so make sure you are not going to get cut off by water flooding in behind you. Fish as long as you can and then move to another rock where you have previously noted the ground to be clean. Hold the rod all the time where possible. You need to know just when the bass has picked up the crab in order to set the hook and get him coming. Remember there are snags all around you. There is no way you can afford to let the bite develop into a 'slack liner' as this gives the bass too much of a chance to drag the lead into a rock and cough the bait out. Even though a bass feeding in such a snaggy environment will give you a good bite, it can still become wary if it feels any undue resistance on the bait.

The second favourite bait for shallow rock fishing is a squid and lugworm cocktail. Thread a lugworm up the shank of the hook and over the eye, nicking a strip of squid on behind. The third choice of bait is a whole king ragworm. You may be unable to buy them from a tackle shop so I'm afraid it's back to the fork and some backache! A whole king rag is a great summertime bait for big bass. To fish these species successfully you have to eliminate as much of the luck factor as possible, although there will always be someone who throws a stale bait 10 yards and hooks a 12 pounder!

Left: When you hook a good bass at a distance, it may come easily at first before plunging into the kelp at the edges of the rock base. Keep your rod up and the pressure on to keep the fish moving all the time.

Go Fishing for Bass

You need to develop a feeling for bass; to learn its temperament, its likes and its dislikes, its habitat and the bait it is likely to be feeding on in the area you are fishing. The time of year, state of the tide, time of day and the influx of freshwater from streams that may make regional salinity changes all need to be carefully monitored. The bass angler has a difficult task and devotees to the sport are usually single-minded in their pursuit and respect what they hunt. Personally I rate shore fishing more highly than boat fishing although boat fishing can be far more productive. When shore fishing, you do everything yourself: collect bait, find an area, cast out, hook, fight and beach the fish. You can rightfully call that bass your own. With a roaring surf, screaming birds and a backdrop of sand dunes or mountains, fishing for bass has a magnificence all of its own.

GO FISHING FOR

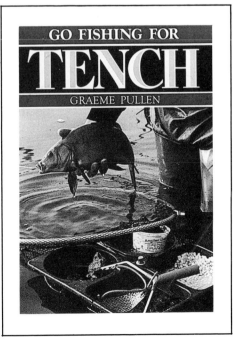

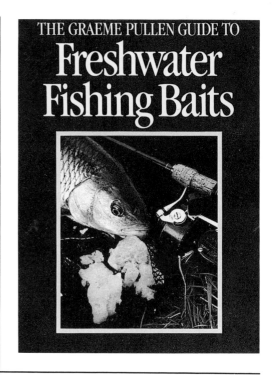
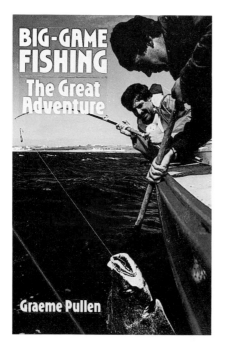